DEPOSIT INSURANCE: THEORY, POLICY AND EVIDENCE

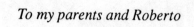

To my parents and Roberto

DEPOSIT INSURANCE: THEORY, POLICY AND EVIDENCE

Rita Carisano

Dartmouth

Aldershot · Brookfield USA · Hong Kong · Singapore · Sydney

© Rita Carisano 1992

Published by
Dartmouth Publishing Company Limited
Gower House
Croft Road
Aldershot
Hants GU11 3HR

Dartmouth Publishing Company Limited
Distributed in the United States by
Ashgate Publishing Company
Old Post Road
Brookfield
Vermont 05036
USA

A CIP catalogue record for this book is available from the British Library and the US Library of Congress

368.854
C27d

ISBN 185521 174 2

m.f.
Laserset by Computype Manuscript Services, Standard House, 49 Lawrence Street, York
Printed in Great Britain by
Billing & Sons Ltd, Worcester

Contents

List of tables

List of figures

Introduction

Since the pioneering experience of the U.S.A., many countries have adopted some form of a deposit insurance scheme to reimburse depositors in the event of a bank failure.

The ghosts of the wide-spread banking panics and the domino-fashion failures of the '30s have been long-hanging over the political choices of monetary authorities. The final aim of every intervention in financial markets, hence, has been that of preventing the crisis of a single bank from compromising the stability and the performance of the economic system as a whole.

Even when the ghosts have lost vigour, the actual possibility of bank runs remained, providing an incentive to introduce protective instruments within the financial system's institutional framework.

Deposit insurance schemes have been a response to this incentive.

At the present, while deregulation is fashionable, deposit insurance contributes to preserve the stability of the banking industry by protecting unsophisticated savers without, on the other hand, affecting competition.

In the last years many countries have set up deposit insurance schemes; the U.S. are now thinking of reshaping theirs. Also the European Community has adopted an official Recommendation regarding the deposit guarantee issue. Member States are requested to conform either their existing or their projected deposit insurance systems to some common features.

The favour bank deposit insurance meets derives from its very nature and from its peculiarities.

Although deposit insurance is viewed as an interference in the financial market, it is not properly a form of banks' regulation. Rather, it is a device conceived as a component of the institutional financial framework. It is not necessarily imposed by monetary authorities, and sometimes voluntary arrangements exist that are equally effective in protecting deposits and in raising the public confidence in the banking industry exist. Furthermore, deposit insurance is a quite flexible device in the sense that different schemes may be planned in order to adjust the operative aspects of the guarantee, according to the single banking industry.

In spite of this special and appealing nature, some issues arise which have been widely discussed by economists, with the ambitious aim to find a compromise between an ideal deposit insurance scheme and its feasibility.

Firstly, the operative aspects and therefore the effectiveness of deposit insurance are closely linked to the interrelation existing with other different forms of protection of the banking industry. Tradition, experience and political choices are crucial for the extension of regulation over financial activities. However, the regulation of banks' activities, supervision and the microeconomic functions of central banks as lenders of last resort play an essential role within most financial systems and therefore deposit insurance acts within a regulated environment. In many cases regulation itself supports deposit-guarantee schemes in that it limits the incentives these provide in terms of banks' moral hazard, becoming a complementary aspect of the insurance.

A basic trade-off exists between the benefits of financial stability and the costs of a possible misallocation of resources associated with excessive risk-taking induced by deposit insurances.

Secondly, different views exist about the nature of banking panics and of financial instability providing competitive rationales for deposit insurance. Furthermore, over time new sources of instability have arisen, concerning interbank relations rather than banks' inherent weaknesses. At present, a danger may arrive from the payment system whenever a large participant defaults on its payments, thus making other banks insolvent. To be actually effective in minimising banking panics risk deposit insurance schemes have to be prepared to face also these eventualities.

The aim of this book is to analyse all the points concerning deposit) insurance in order to provide insight for further discussion. However, the backdrop of the following analysis is that an ideal deposit insurance system, providing deposit protection and financial stability at the same extent in every banking environment, does not exist. Nevertheless, deposit insurance can be adapted in a flexible manner to the peculiar features of different financial systems and then it can be usefully utilised to appropriately pursue stability objectives in every environment.

1 Banks and deposit insurance

The starting point in dealing with deposit insurance has to be founded on the relation existing between the latter and the banking system.

The intrinsic instability of the banking system is the main reason that has lead authorities in the past and present to provide the financial structure with protective instruments. Bank runs and panics are costly in social and economic terms and must be avoided for the welfare of the system as a whole.

For this reason banking regulations can be viewed as a government response to a crisis in the banking system and presumably each regulatory framework created is based on a model that explains the origin of banking panic.[1] Nevertheless, whatever the model underling monetary policy, each regulation measure – including deposit insurance – aims to protect banks' economic functions.

The banking industry is unanimously considered as providing unique services by combining the holding of illiquid assets with the issuing of liquid liabilities. In spite of – and indeed because of – this unique function, banks are susceptible to disruptive deposit runs, because depositors are able to withdraw their deposits either on demand or on short notice and bank assets cannot be sold quickly enough without losses for meeting depositors claims that exceed bank reserves.

This chapter analyses the economics of banks to show that, compared with all types of businesses "banking is different", and that banking crises – when widespread – adversely affect the financial system's performance. They reduce the supply of money, by raising the cost of credit intermediation[2] and reduce the efficiency of the credit allocation process.

The high costs of banking runs and their panic inducing potential are the rationale for the existing safety net established in most countries. In this net, deposit insurance and the central bank, as lender of last resort, and the regulations of bank activities, operate together to provide an institutional environment aimed at stabilising the banking system by preventing runs and panics.

Our purpose is to characterise the role played by deposit insurance inside the safety net, in particular towards the lender of last resort. This relation is crucial, although the two instruments act differently in dealing with bank industry protection. In practice they support each other to safeguard the stability of the financial system and preserve economic development.

1.1 BANKS AS SPECIAL FIRMS

According to the theory of finance, commercial banks are firms which provide two main distinct services, as Fama (1980) argued. A bank's first function is related to both the maintenance of a system of account and the exchange of deposits and other forms of wealth for currency. Banks facilitate transactions by providing payment transmission services. The second major function of banks is portfolio management. They issue deposits and use the proceeds to purchase securities.

In the first part of this book we analyse the latter function of banks, in order to point out the unique role they play by allowing depositors' wealth to meet investment opportunities at a low level of information and monitoring costs. This is the main and traditional argument for establishing a deposit insurance scheme, although in the second chapter we shall see that the payment system service is also crucial to the case for banking protection.

Portfolio management is essential for understanding banks' unique economic role because it combines illiquid assets and liquid liabilities in one entity.

Banks satisfy depositor liquidity needs by issuing deposits. Those meeting these liquidity needs with less liquid assets make more funds available to support productive illiquid investments. In reality, banks borrow from individuals – depositors – and lend to entrepreneurs who need to raise capital for investment projects.

Following the reasoning of Diamond and Dybvig (1986) it is possible to deal with banks' role as intermediaries by analysing their balance sheets, where liabilities and assets are combined together to serve as an economic function and not just to provide a record of book-keeping entries.

We shall focus on a bank with a very simplified balance sheet:

$$L + R = D + K$$

where   L = loans;
        R = required cash reserve;
        D = deposits;
        K = owners equity.

This balance sheet neglects all other items which although fundamental for banking activity, are not necessary to describe the economic function of banks as unique intermediaries.[3]

The main items of the two sides of the balance sheet described above – loans and deposits – have very different features: loans are non marketable and illiquid, deposits are liquid and redeemable at par.

Loans are the banks' distinguishing item in that creating a bank loan requires borrowers and lenders to find one another, and for lenders to evaluate and monitor potential borrowers. In creating bank loans, banks perform a value-adding activity. In fact, monitoring borrowers and information production about credit risks are bank activities which cannot be replicated by capital markets. In the lending process banks gather information in both evaluating the loan – they face the adverse selection problem of assessing the quality of potential borrowers – and in monitoring the borrower after a loan is made, in order to control his behaviour towards a morally hazardous attitude. Banks provide a unique service by gaining expertise in these ex-ante and ex-post information gathering activities.

The cost of gathering information about borrowers, current and future circumstances and the difficulty borrowers have in transmitting information about their creditworthiness prevent both individual borrowers and lenders from meeting. Furthermore, even though an individual investor could gather information by himself there would be an economic and inefficient duplication of these efforts and an insufficient monitoring to uphold the value of the loan.[4]

The point that the centralization of ownership and information collection in a diversified financial intermediary provides a real service, has been made by many.[5] In his paper Diamond (1984) has developed a theory of financial intermediation based on minimizing the cost of monitoring information which is useful for solving incentive problems between borrowers and lenders. Diamond argues that a financial intermediary – a bank – has a net cost advantage related to direct lending and borrowing and that the key of this net advantage is the diversification within the intermediary. In Diamond's model a financial intermediary raises funds from many lenders (depositors), promises him a pattern of returns, lends to entrepreneurs and spends resources monitoring and enforcing loan contracts. In this environment the financial intermediary monitors entrepreneurs information, and receives payments from the entrepreneurs which is not observed by depositors; depositors in the model – in line with reality – delegate monitoring to the intermediary. Diamond demonstrates that as an intermediary deals with an increasing number of borrowers and lenders, contracting costs decline monotonically, that is costs of delegation approach zero as the number of loans to entrepreneurs grows without bound.[6] The result is that no other delegated monitoring structure will have lower costs and it provides a positive role for financial intermediaries.

An interesting implication of Diamond's delegated monitoring model is that the intermediary's assets will be illiquid. This is because the intermediary is delegated the task of observing information about each loan which no one else but the borrower observes. The intermediary contracts to hold them rather than to sell them. If loans were sold, monitoring and enforcement would also have to be transferred to someone else and the buyer would have to incur in monitoring costs again, duplicating the efforts of the first intermediary. Assets are illiquid because banks have private information about their quality and because in most cases they are a highly personal and confidential affair between the borrower – the entrepreneur- and the lender – the bank.[7] Furthermore, if loans could be sold, the originating intermediary would not face an incentive to monitor or produce information. The only way of ensuring that financial intermediaries undertake their unique role is by forcing them to maintain the ownership of the loans they create.

Thus, banks have as their principal assets the loans, which are not marketable and are illiquid. Moreover, banks provide a unique service by specializing in gathering information and monitoring borrowers. Banks reduce the costs of finding profitable investments in the productive projects developed by private entrepreneurs.

Nevertheless, the unique role that banks play is also related to their intermediation between borrowers and depositors. Banks are unique institutions because they provide services on each side of the balance sheet, by combining deposits with loans.

Let us turn to the liability side of banks' balance sheets. Deposits are issued by banks and since they are redeemable at par, they satisfy the liquidity needs of depositors. By issuing deposits, banks create "riskless" securities for trading purposes, that is banks' liabilities are special because they circulate as a medium of exchange.[8]

In this respect banks are unique firms because they create liabilities which are debt whose value is known and represent a riskless security for depositors. Furthermore banks are unique because they back these liabilities with diversified portfolios.

In their seminal paper Diamond and Dybvig (1983) put forward a different definition of liquidity by sustaining that banks are institutions providing insurance against random consumption needs. While agents prefer the high return long-term investment projects, they may want to consume at an early date. Banks, by pooling the long and short-term investments in the right proportion, can issue securities – deposits – which insure against the risk of early consumption.

Although the two meanings of liquidity presented above differ from a theoretical point of view, as we shall see in the second chapter, for the moment they support a similar rationale for sustaining the unique role played by banks. Banks, in fact, are viewed as financial institutions that provide maturity transformation services. The conversion of illiquid loans into liquid deposits is a bank's economic function as a special intermediary, that could not otherwise be obtained. In conclusion we may argue that banks are special firms because they enhance social welfare by funding illiquid assets with very liquid liabilities. Banks provide resources for productive long-run investments, necessary for the development of the economy, by raising funds from individuals through a contract – deposit – that offers them the redemption option at par on demand. Banks combine the interests of enterprises who need capital for risky projects and the interests of depositors who want to lend without losing liquidity.

The liquidity transformation that enables banks to provide useful services, however is also a source of their susceptibility to disruptive deposit runs.

1.2 BANK RUNS AND THEIR COSTS

The peculiar characteristics that enable banks to provide a real economic service by funding illiquid assets with liquid liabilities is at the same time their weakness. This feature can potentially lead them to costly runs and then the financial system to potential instability.

Deposit contract entitles depositors either to withdraw on demand or on short maturity. A bank loan, on the other hand, is non marketable – i.e. it is illiquid – and if the depositors' claims exceed legal and free reserves, banks are forced to sell assets even if they are not mature and notwithstanding the asymmetric information associated with them.[9]

Depositors know that banks operate on a fractional reserve system and that they also operate according to the first come first served rule, so that if for whatever reason depositors expect banks not to be able to discharge all their claims fully and on time, they present them for redemption as soon as possible. If withdrawals are large and sudden, this will force banks to sell some assets.

For the moment we are not interested in analysing which factors cause depositors to change their behaviour and then to withdraw their deposits from banks. As we shall see, two main distinct theoretical lines of argument compete in providing different explanations for the origin of banking runs with consequent different rationales for deposit insurance as a protection device.[10]

Since our purpose is to argue that bank runs are possible and that they impose high social costs, let us suppose here that depositors are induced

9

to withdraw their funds. What distinguishes a normal withdrawal from a withdrawal leading to a bank run is that the latter is so large and wide-scale that the bank is unable to meet depositors' claims on the basis of cash reserves. Furthermore deposit outflows have to occur suddenly, so that the affected bank is unlikely to be able to attract sufficient replenish funds to affect all its losses and it will be forced to sell earning assets. A bank run occurs when banks are induced to manage their assets to face the withdrawals.

Part of the literature on banking instability, namely that based on the analysis of historical experience, focuses on bank panics rather than on bank runs.[11] On the contrary, other authors use the two terms synonymously. In our view they may differ as following. A panic involves a large number of banks and a common lack of confidence in the financial system; a run could be limited locally to a single bank or a few banks. However the difference is neither clear in practice, nor particularly useful from an analytical point of view. In general when dealing with runs or panics, we shall refer to damaging events which affect banks when depositors lose faith in the institutions' ability to provide liquidity transformation services regularly.

The possibility that an extraordinary wide-scale outflow from depositors becomes a bank run is strictly inherent in the structure of the banking industry.

As Goodhart (1985, 1986) has pointed out, if bank assets were liquid, that is their market price were known, there would be a tendency for banks to develop deposit liabilities whose value would vary with the value of the assets, and thus there would be no ground for bank runs. Since assets are illiquid by nature, their value depends on the information that banks have. Banks are forced to provide liabilities which have a nominal value, fixed interest, and a guarantee of being converted into cash at any time. Goodhart argues that the nature of bank assets determines the nature of bank liabilities and the bank's susceptibility to runs.

When depositors suddenly rush to withdraw their deposits and a run occurs, social welfare is negatively affected. This is the main argument in favour of government intervention in depositor institutions. The major social benefits deposit insurance are intended to provide is the prevention of widespread bank deposit runs and, in general protection of the economy.

Bank runs impose social costs affecting output in different ways. The most traditional of them was pointed out by Friedman and Schwartz (1963) in their famous work. By analysing past bank runs in the United States they argued that the banks' difficulties made the general contraction of the economy worse, by leading to a rapid fall in the supply of money. In their view the damage to the money supply process caused by bank runs affects the real economy.

As later Bernanke (1983) showed, the monetary channel specified by Friedman and Schwartz for the transmission of negative effects from the financial to the real sector does not completely exhaust the damages done by bank runs. By focusing the attention on the credit allocation of banks rather than on their function in multiplying money, Bernanke argued that the financial crises of the past were socially costly in terms of output contraction, because they destroyed an important conduit of investment funds in the economy. The disruptions of 1930-33 reduced the effectiveness of the financial sector as a whole in performing market making and information gathering services.

Thus, the special feature of banks as intermediaries between borrowers and lenders, allows to identify banks' susceptibility to crises and their costs in terms of reduction in real production. Banking crises raise the cost of bank intermediation services, that is the cost of channelling funds from the depositors to productive projects carried on by entrepreneurs. As Bernanke argues, banks choose operating procedures that minimize the cost of credit intermediation. Thus, banking troubles affect the intermediation performed by banks and hence allocation efficiency and impose high social costs. A bank experiencing a run may be forced to sell its assets on the spot. Premature liquidation of loans has immediate adverse effects on economic activity. Production and consumption plans are consequently frustrated.

The information problems associated with bank assets also play an important role in making runs particularly costly for social welfare. On this subject Murton (1989) has underlined the existing discontinuity in value of bank assets when moving from states of the world in which assets are allowed to mature to states in which assets are liquidated. This lag between the "going-concern" value and the liquidation value is a critical point in explaining why bank runs are costly.

As we have seen bank assets are uncertain in value because of the information and monitoring relation involved which set the market price.

The centralized ownership of loans by banks is a fundamental element of their real value. If a bank is forced to sell some assets quickly, the value of information gathering and monitoring activities is likely to be lost.

To analyse this point let us define the two main prices associated with every loan. The first price is the equilibrium value, that is the price obtainable given normal search time for the highest bidder on the market.[12] The second price indicates the immediate market value of the loan and it is called "fire-sale" value. In reality the equilibrium market price does not represent the true value of the loan. Rather it is the price that is recorded on the bank's books when market value accounting is used and a "reasonable" search time is assumed. On the other hand the "fire-sale" price is a lower limit on the obtainable price, as it can be obtained almost immediately without significant search. The spread between the two prices is a function of the amount of search required to evaluate the information and monitoring components of the asset as precisely as possible. Again this amount depends on the uniqueness or the marketability of the asset, on the market fluidity, and of the number of net sellers of the same asset.[13]

The relationship between the equilibrium market value and the fire-sale market value of two securities is shown in Figure 1.1 where the former price is considered to be the same for the two assets and their marketability to be different. Security A is more liquid than B, so that it requires less information and the spread between its two prices is, at any time, less than the spread between the equilibrium market value and the fire-sale market value of security B. Security B has, at any time, a lower fire-sale price. This means that the losses that a bank faces by selling its securities on the spot depends upon their marketability and on the banks portfolio composition.

In terms of cost, the losses a bank may suffer by selling its securities at fire-sale prices are socially prominent, because in the process creditworthy borrowers lose financing. Furthermore, a fire-sale liquidation of bank assets forces a market valuation of assets that otherwise is not spontaneously provided by market forces.

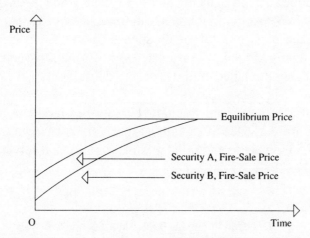

Figure 1.1: Relationship between the fire-sale market price of two
securities, A and B, and their equilibrium market price

1.3 BANK FAILURES AND RUNS TO OTHER BANKS: THE CASES FOR DEPOSIT INSURANCE

The losses a bank suffers in a fire-sale liquidation of its assets also has relevance to its internal equilibrium. The losses in the sale of assets is charged against its net worth.

Among the major hazards typically faced by banks (such as bad assets, overbanking, mismanagement) illiquidity is the most frequent reason for bank failures.

Following Tussing's (1967) analysis, it is possible and useful to distinguish two sources of illiquidity: errors in judgement by bank management and lack of confidence in the banking system. If withdrawals are large enough to cause severe liquidity problems for their bank, the latter will incur a failure. When a bank has reduced its normal inventory of liquid assets to satisfy claims, it must begin to liquidate its illiquid assets in a "fire-sale". The severity of a liquidity problem faced by a bank could be viewed in terms of the difference between the equilibrium price and the fire-sale prices of the assets in liquidation. As long as this difference is smaller than the bank market net worth, the bank does not become insolvent, and therefore does not fail.

13

In economic terms, a bank becomes insolvent when the market value of its equity falls to zero. In this case, the present value of its total assets is equal to the present value of its deposit and non-deposit liabilities other than equity capital.[14] However, even if a bank is economically insolvent, it does not failed until it is declared insolvent by the regulatory authorities.

The relation between bank liquidity and solvency problems, connected through the present value of capital, has been clearly shown by Benston et al. (1986) in terms of condition for bank liquidity and solvency. These are outlined in Table 1.1.

Table 1.1: Conditions for Bank Liquidity and Solvency

Bank liquid and solvent	$A=A^*>D$ $K=K^*>0$	where:	A = equilibrium market value of assets
Bank facing liquidity problem but solvent	$A>A^*>D$ $K>K^*>0$		A^* = fire-sale market value of assets
Bank facing liquidity problem that induces solvency problem	$A>D>A^*$ $K>0>K^*$		D = market value of deposits (and credit other than capital)
Bank facing fundamental solvency problem	$D>A>A^*$ $0>K>K^*$		K^* = fire-sale value of capital

If a bank run drives an economically solvent bank into insolvency, depositors' losses may increase the uncertainty about the soundness of the banking system. The effects of a bank run on other banks and on the economy depend on the depositors behaviour when they withdraw their funds from the bank that gives rise to the initial run.

Depositors have three alternatives: 1) they can redeposit their funds at another bank perceived as safer; 2) they can purchase perceived safer securities, e.g Treasury securities; 3) they can hold the funds in the form of currency outside the banking system.

The first alternative implies that depositors' fears are restricted only to one bank or to a small number of banks. Depositors withdraw their funds from the institutions perceived to be in financial difficulties and transfer them to other banks. The net result of this operation is just a reshuffling of deposits and reserves within the banking system with no change in the aggregate value of liquidity. Under these conditions the bank run is not contagious to the rest of the system even if its not costless. To the extent that the troubled bank calls in loans, the borrower-lender relations are interrupted; due to the fact that they depend on the private information, it is difficult to replicate them without economic and social costs.[15]

The second alternative implies a greater loss of depositors' faith by in the banking system. In this case depositors use their funds to purchase securities that they believe to be safer substitutes for deposits and create a "flight to quality". In this scenario the sellers of securities are expected to inject the funds back into the banking system, providing an indirect redeposit. In this case, costs associated with a likely rise of interest rates – induced by the growing demand for securities – are added to the renegotiation of called loans. However, this it is not the case for a system-wide contagious run.

If depositors choose the third alternative, namely a flight to currency, the draining of reserves from the system raises the number of bank fire sale insolvencies and makes liquidity problems more likely to be transformed into solvency problems. Banks are likely to raise their reserve ratio to be able to meet sudden deposit claims. The resulting smaller deposit-reserve multiplier intensifies the multiple contraction of money and credit. Borrowers are no longer able to benefit from the intermediation services provided by banks, and the channel of funding is interrupted. The faith in the banking systems is at its lowest and bank failure will become contagious.

This is the panic scenario, that is destabilising for the financial sector and affects the aggregate economic activity. The costs of this scenario are the highest for society.

The maintenance of confidence in the banking system, and soundness and efficiency of individual financial institutions constitute the double argument that justifies public concern. In particular, the costs associated with a single bank failure, and the costs associated with potential system-wide panics, are the foundations a deposit insurance scheme. In this sense deposit insurance is a device to handle banking crises within the institutional framework set up for protecting the financial system.

1.4 DEPOSIT INSURANCE IN A FINANCIAL FRAMEWORK

Deposit insurance is not the only mechanism through which the banking industry can be protected against difficulties. Rather, it is a part of a comprehensive safety net in which other instruments work with the same purpose of protecting the stability of the credit system. In most countries this net is usually founded on three main mechanisms:

1) Last-resort lending
2) Deposit insurance
3) Regulation

The relation among these mechanisms is one of interaction so that it is often difficult to distinguish their single effects and/or identify their single contribution. This occurs also because monetary authorities let them operate jointly. The three instruments supplement each other providing a guarantee for the whole financial system.

Regulation, together with supervision is useful to control and limit bank risk-taking. The purpose of regulation is that of establishing norms for sound banking practices. Capital requirements, portfolio regulations, interest rate ceilings, reserved requirements are the most common constraints imposed by authorities on the banks' activity.

Deposit insurance, which is aimed at increasing confidence by protecting the depositor, does not operate properly without regulation: it might constitute a mechanism with dangerous perverse effects on the behaviour of banks towards risk, and on financial stability. On the other hand, if regulation is too strict, banks will operate away from efficiency objectives. Thus the last-resort lending function of central banks allows banks to behave according to efficiency criteria without letting them incur into self-fulfilling runs.

Our purpose here is to present some aspects of deposit insurance as an instrument operating to protect depositors if bank runs occur. Furthermore, an analysis of the crucial relation existing between deposit insurance and last resort lending is developed in order to clarify the role played by deposit insurance in the financial framework.

1.4.1 Deposit insurance

The major justification for deposit insurance from monetary authorities' point of view is that of reducing the external diseconomies resulting from bank failures. These externalities[16] can be divided into micro and macro-externalities. The formers concern the single agents and justify deposit insurance in order to protect small depositors, to increase competitive equality between different size banks and to protect the bank as a financial intermediary playing a unique role in the system. On the contrary, the macro externalities view deposit insurance aimed at preventing the deleterious effects that contagious bank runs could have on the money supply and the payment system.

The small depositors protection argument for deposit insurance is one of the most direct ones. "Small depositor" is considered to be one who is generally incapable of fully understanding bank risk and who may over react to rumours concerning a bank's solvency. Furthermore small depositors are thought to be more seriously affected by losses incurred in a bank run. In this case deposit insurance is intended to protect the naive behaviour of depositors who want to have a reasonable rate of return, but need safety first and liquidity. By protecting these unsophisticated depositors deposit insurance intends to prevent bank runs occurring because of rumours.

Deposit insurance may also contribute to competitive equality between different banks. In absence of an effective protection system, large banks might be viewed as inherently safer than smaller ones. In this sense deposit insurance is a device to improve competitive efficiency in the banking system.   The argument that deposit insurance scheme protects financial intermediation is the strongest one among the micro economic objectives. As we have seen it prevents the crucial connection between the financial and the real system from breaking off.

Net currency outflows from the banking system cause unexpected fluctuations in the aggregate stock of money resulting in a reduction of money supply, and consequently in economic recession and depression.

Banks serve another fundamental function as much as they help regulate payments among agents. A single bank failure could have serious transmission effects involving agents in a systemic risk because of interbank transactions.

Several countries have established explicit schemes for deposit insurance which are similar among them. They differ for membership (voluntary or compulsory) coverage (in the majority of the schemes there is a formal cutoff point for insurance coverage), administration (private or governmental) funding, (actuarially or based on special ex-post levies), but they all have the common goal of guaranteeing pay-offs to insured depositors in the event of banks failure.

Furthermore, all central banks and monetary authorities potentially and actually act in order to prevent depositors from losing their funds, providing a de facto, or implicit, insurance.

Most of the existing schemes operate by setting up a fund out of which depositors' claims are met. Member banks are charged a premium that is usually a flat rate on the amount of assessable deposits. If a bank fails and it is declared insolvent, the insurance fund protects deposit accounts usually up to a certain ceiling.

The United States deposit insurance scheme (Fdic), which is the oldest of those established after the '30s and the most attractive from a theoretical point of view. Reference to this scheme may be found in many other ones. The U.S. scheme has been subsequently introduced in different countries. According to its structure, the Federal deposit insurance system provides protection for the first $ 100,000 of each domestic deposit account. In return member banks, which are commercial banks, face a flat premium. If a bank failure occurs, after the declaration of insolvency by the chartering agency, the Fidc is appointed receiver and exercises its insurance powers; it may dispose of the assets and pay off creditors.[17] The practical manner in which the Fdic settles failed banks, that is by providing a de facto 100 %, provides an insurance cover to most depositors and general creditors; this moves the instrument from its original statement and objectives. However the U.S. scheme is a system of deposit protection that is closest to an insurance scheme.

This point is of great relevance in dealing with deposit insurance. Among the instruments established to guarantee financial market stability, deposit insurance programmes are thought as being in keeping with explicit devices; on the contrary, the intervention of central monetary authorities is implicit in the more general task they pursue and discretionary.

In principle the nature of deposit insurance is that of an insurance contract where the insurer – agency – promises to third party beneficiaries – depositors – that they will be wholly reimbursed in the event that the parties carrying the insurance – banks – do not redeem deposits. According to this insurance contract, deposit insurance uses some typical tools to protect itself against risk. It establishes rules for the applicability of the insurance, collects information on the likely risks that the insured parties will impose on it, practises coinsurance,[18] limits the amount of the insurance offered to the insured.

Nevertheless, all the existing deposits insurance systems, are not proper insurance. As they are mostly structured on the model of insurance contract, they are not insurances at all, but rather financial guarantees for depositors' accounts.

In the deposit insurance scheme the terms of an insurance contract described below are not respected. In providing its insurance, the insurance agency fund guarantees the account holders to redeem their deposits if the insured institution fails to meet its obligations. In substance this contract identifies three different beneficiaries of the insurance: the single insured depositor, the financial system as a whole, and finally banks.

Depositors are the first beneficiaries of the insurance. Their credit is directly protected by the agency even if only partially because of the coinsurance provision. The second beneficiary implicit in every deposit guarantee scheme is the financial system. Given the political nature of insurance systems, in fact, the main objective they pursue is the stability and soundness of the banking sector. To protect the system, however, means to protect banks as well. Thus banks are the third beneficiary of the guarantee provided by the deposit insurance. Furthermore, deposit insurance is a *suis generis* insurance because in providing the claims arising from a damaging event and in preventing this event, as it is for any other insurance, the second element, that of prevention, is prevailing. Deposit insurance is intended more to prevent bank runs rather than to indemnify depositors. Insuring a bank and its deposits prevents the effects of a potentially contagious run in the financial system. Specifically, deposit insurance aims to allow unsound banks to leave the banking industry, while protecting the banking system against widespread panics.

But the deposit insurance scheme is different from a typical insurance contract in a more fundamental sense. The nature of the risk to be insured against by deposit insurance is different from the risk facing other kinds of insurance. The probability of a bank failure is not the same actuarial category as the probability of death, illness, fire or car accident. In these cases the probability of the risk to occur is determinable and then measurable in terms of a fair premium for the insurance. On the contrary, the risk of bank failure is difficult to determine and to price.

Even if more developed actuarial bases were provided, there is at the moment a great difficulty in measuring the risk of failure for banking firms. This comes from the interaction of microeconomic policy in conjunction with the legal and institutional structure of the banking system. As Goodhart (1987) pointed out, this interaction affects the probability of bank failure.

Consequently, it is quite hard to identify an actuarially sound systems of risk-related premiums for deposit insurance. In this respect, deposit insurance schemes do not have access to an other fundamental insurance tool, that is pricing the premiums according to the risk. The evidence which indicates this is the flat rate premiums which are charged to banks in the existing systems. As we shall see, recent works have approached this problem by applying the option pricing analysis, and have proposed some reform for the deposit insurance premiums. For the moment these proposals remain impracticable for some reasons we will focus on later.

At present, the mispricing of premiums, compared with the risk imposed by investment and net worth position of banks, asks for rigid regulatory and supervisory activities by the insurers. To the extent that insurers are unable to gather sufficient information about the true net worth and true risk undertaken by their insured banks – because of asymmetric information problems associated with the special nature of banking firms – a rigid regulation structure is needed to protect the insurance system against moral hazard on behalf of banks. Historical experience supports the existing relation between the introduction of deposit insurance and increasing regulation. This regulation has been viewed as being the indirect cost of a deposit insurance present in the financial system.[19]

One more typical insurance tool remains unused in deposit insurance. An insurance company can limit the amount of insurance offered to an insured. In principle, this device could be available in the case of deposit insurance, for example, by placing limits on the growth of liabilities in under capitalised institutions.[20] In practice the aim of protecting the financial system on the whole prevails in the determination of run-

associated features of deposit insurance systems, raising the distance from a typical insurance scheme.[21]

In a first best world, where information asymmetries do not exist and the social welfare function is fully identified, a socially optimal deposit insurance scheme could be established. In this framework the insurer would guarantee all deposits and set a premium (p_i) for each bank equal to the ex-ante social costs of its failure, where the social costs of failure reflect the private ones adjusted for administrative costs and externalities. This optimal scheme could reduce the probability of bank panics, with their associated real sector impact, while minimising any resource misallocation costs resulting from the supply of the insurance. It should act in order to allow the exit of unsound institutions from the banking industry, while protecting both the stability of the banking system, avoiding widespread runs, and making back risk-taking neither subsidized nor inefficiently discouraged.[22]

Assuming the described environment for a risk-neutral insurer, the single bank premium (p_i) providing the optimal insurance scheme would be:

$$p_i = l_i(\theta_i) + C_i(\gamma_i) + e_i$$

where: l_i = expected insurer loss associated with the ith bank failure within the premium-setting period;

θ_i = vector of risk characteristics of the ith bank;

$C_i(\gamma_i)$ = cost function reflecting the insurer monitoring surveillance and auditing costs (γ_i);

e_1 = some social cost adjustment to the private costs of insurance provision to account for externalities.

Compared with the existing pricing scheme associated to the most of insurance systems, that is:

$$p_i = KD_i$$

where K: = constant charge applied to all banks independently of their risk characteristics;

D_i = deposit amount of ith bank.

21

The social welfare maximizing pricing scheme appears to be very far from being realized in practice.

The ideal technical deposit insurance scheme should eliminate that portion of market-determined risk premium reflecting the threat of bank runs without altering the portion reflecting the other risks.[23]

The achievement of this result would retain all market discipline exercised in absence of a deposit insurance, but without the social costs of bank runs.

In reality the existing deposit insurance schemes are far from an ideal system. Moreover providing their multiprotection, they benefit from the interaction with other instruments, in particular with the presence of the last resort lending function of central banks.

1.4.2 Lender of last resort and deposit insurance

Lender of last resort (Llr) function is one of the central banks' responsibilities. In this respect, it constitutes both a monetary policy instrument and a means to provide liquidity to single banks facing temporary difficulties in converting deposits at par into currency.

As we have seen, the banking system needs a central bank because of its Llr function which enables institutions to honour their obligation of convertibility. Indeed, the establishment of the central banks has been justified by the historical experience of most countries, and the need to provide a bank of the banks that stabilise the system against runs and panics.

Moreover the United States' example indicates the establishment of the Federal Reserve as a legitimization of the Llr function carried on by a super parties institution and the institution of the federal insurance system (Fdic) as a solution to the insufficient Llr behaviour of the Fed during the panic periods of the '30s. The reluctancy of the Fed to operate as Llr meant that intervention was not large enough to moderate banks' runs by replenishing reserve losses and by reestablishing banks' credibility; the deposit insurance was viewed as a necessary complement to the Fed in maintaining the integrity of the banking system. As we shall see, this complementarity is undoubted and very effective in pursuing the goal of the financial stability. Nevertheless the two instruments are intended to operate in different circumstances according to different immediate aims and different technical aspects. A deposit insurance system, contrary to a Llr, is not directly involved in the political concern of the central authorities. The central bank could face circumstances in which soundness of the Llr objective and monetary policy goals are incompatible.

Deposit insurance on the contrary, is established and works to protect savers against losses of deposits and to protect the banking system against widespread withdrawals. In this sense the presence of a deposit insurance system could be viewed as a device for restricting the need for the central bank assistance through the discount window. In this, a more restricted and straight goal of deposit insurance is possible to identify a fundamental difference between the two instruments. Their differences, however, concern many other aspects related to their different nature: deposit insurance is a guarantee against losses arising from certain events, whereas the lending of last resort is a particular performance of the central bank. Deposit insurance operates according to its scheme, whereas Llr assistance is provided according to contingent judgements of the monetary authority. Deposit insurance honours its obligations with resources from its funds whereas Llr injects reserves in the banking system either through the purchase of securities – open market operations – or loans to banks.

On the basis of these observations a useful paradigm could be derived that helps distinguishing the two instruments under analysis and makes their relationship clearer.

According to these paradigms we can define deposit insurance mechanism as:

1. Explicit
2. Non-Discretionary
3. Ex-ante
4. Limited
5. Costless for the community

Deposit insurance guarantee is explicit in the sense that it is part of a well defined ad hoc scheme. If a bank failure occurs, depositors are aware that the insurance system's task is to make their deposits safe and that it will do so. The Llr function of the central bank could be as effective as deposit insurance in protecting deposits, but its guarantee is

23

contingent and there is no certainty about it. The Llr's involvement in a bank trouble does not find its rationale in a statutory provision. Deposit insurance, on the contrary, is provided explicitly to avoid negative consequences of banks' failure. Convertibility of deposits into currency is assured, if not by the bank through by the deposit insurance.

Llr is not only an implicit mean for preventing runs, it is also discretionary, whereas deposit insurance is non discretionary. The Llr's operating depends on central banks judgements regarding the solvency of the bank experiencing the run. On the other hand, deposit insurance guarantee is automatic. The payoff of the insured deposit is a specific commitment of deposit insurance in the event of bank failure.

Llr's supply of money or purchase of securities is a non predictable behaviour of a central bank. The likelihood that Llr's intervention will be viewed as necessary, and the conditions under which it will occur depend on the assets structure of the banking system. Depositors, who do not have access to this information, cannot make fair forecasts on the Llr's behaviour, that is they cannot know ex-ante the Llr's decision concerning a bank support.

In this regard the decision to get involved itself in a bank failure offers to depositors an ex-post guarantee. Credible depositor insurance eliminates the initial reason for banking runs by making depositors' expectations certain. The probable commitment of the Llr to make deposits safe is not an effective means in preventing financial instability arising from depositor's withdrawals and it is not effective in reducing depositors fears.

This uncertainty about the Llr's intervention and its consequences on depositors' behaviour has stimulated the identification of different circumstances that require deposit insurance guarantee rather than Llr's guarantee.

In the most classical distinction,[24] last resorting lending and deposit insurance face different aspects of potential crisis situations.

Llr should provide direct assistance to institutions that are economically solvent, but are experiencing a liquidity crisis. In this concern the lending of last resort from the central bank is justified in that it can provide time for the bank to restructure its balance equilibrium. A temporary liquidity default can be resolved by the central bank emergency lending to the troubled institution. The ready access to central bank credit allows the bank subject to deposit withdrawal to avoid costly

24

negotiations with other private institutions. By reducing this cost last resort lending permits individual banks to operate both with less liquidity and capital than they would otherwise need and if the commitment of the Llr is strong enough, depositors are assured on the banks' capacity to continue being solvent.

Deposit insurance, instead, faces bank failure. A bank declared insolvent is managed by the insurance agency and depositors are refunded according to the insurance scheme.

This approach looks at Llr and deposit insurance as instruments facing two distinct bank situations: illiquidity and insolvency. As it has been pointed out by many authors[25] it is often not possible to determine whether the problem a bank is experiencing is one of illiquidity or of insolvency. The distinction is unclear per se and sometimes the emergency credit provided by the Llr makes it less clear.

If a bank is receiving such emergency funds it has presumably been rationed out of the ordinary market – the other financial intermediaries or private lenders have refused to lend to it at any finite price – and therefore such a bank is not readily distinguished from one that is solvent.[26] On the other hand, if the market opinion is that the bank is undoubtedly solvent, it should not have to apply to last resort lending to meet its obligations and the market could fund it. Finally, there is a possibility that a bank can face insolvency problems without the market and the central bank recognising it.

The emergency credit provided by the Llr can not be viewed as strictly and exclusively related to illiquidity events. The difficulty to identify this in practice requires a discretional judgement by the central bank when a bank is in trouble. In this sense the distinction between illiquidity and insolvency does not provide a useful criteria to separate the field of Llr from that of deposit insurance intervention. For this reason alternative distinctions have been suggested to make clear when a central bank intervention is appropriate for a bank's trouble.

The fair role of the government in providing funds as Llr could arise, as Kanatas (1986) pointed out, from the request of emergency credit because of depositors' risk-aversion. If a bank is so severely impaired that even risk-neutral depositors would attempt to withdraw their money, the Llr should not provide credit to the bank, in order to not support an insolvent institution. On the contrary, if depositors show their risk aversion, then, when providing credit the Llr is merely substituting itself for a risk-neutral private lender, and this represents a temporary facility until private lending by less risk-adverse depositors can be arranged.

Probably, in practice, this distinction is not much more useful then the former one, based on liquidity and insolvency. Distinguishing risk-neutral and risk-averse depositors withdrawals could be difficult.

Another proposal shifts the problem from the single bank's trouble to the nature of the run.[27] In considering the different roles of deposit insurance and central bank in protecting depositors, bank failures could be divided into two categories: normal and depression ones. The former occur in normal economic and financial circumstances, the latter in depressed conditions, when banks become insolvent due to a sharp recession.

Normal failures arise from mismanagement and shifts in the local population. They are conjunctural events and are a legitimate concern of a deposit insurance system. On the contrary, depression failures find their causes in the economic downturn that occurs if proper action by central bank and fiscal authorities is not pursued. In this case Llr has to provide an adequate supply of liquidity to avoid a widespread run and probably a panic. In this view the state of the economy becomes relevant to select the fair means to deal with bank runs. Generally a poor economic scene is considered as evidence of poor monetary and fiscal control so that Llr's assistance to a large number of institutions is a device to remedy for previous defaults. This argument nevertheless considers Llr's assistance strictly linked to the monetary responsibilities of central banks. The burden between Llr' functions as a monetary policy instrument and as an emergency credit firms becomes confused. Whereas, in our view, it is important to allow them to be separate with different goals and different motives.

After this discussion about the different criteria to justify the Llr or the deposit insurance guarantee let us go back to our paradigm. After having defined deposit insurance as explicit, non discretionary and as an ex-ante safe instrument for depositors we have to point out two other aspects: it is limited and costless for the community.

It is limited in the sense that the extent to which its guarantee is provided is limited according to the insurance scheme, as fixed in the establishing statute. The value of the intervention has a ceiling depending on the given amount of guaranteed deposits and the guaranteed percentage of them. Llr's ex-post guarantee has no institutional constraints except on its extent the central bank's estimation on the creation of reserves and thus of money supply. In theory its intervention in market tension might have no limit with respect to monetary policy objectives.

The last characteristic is that a deposit insurance charges the costs of bank failures to the banking system and to the agents involved in it. Llr instead, because of its nature and its ratio charges the community thereby tax payers support. To be insured by the established system, banks have to pay a premium that contributes to the creation of the insurance funds. A failure that triggers off the insurance guarantee imposes its costs only on the banking system. The risk-taking agents – banks – are directly involved in the effects of their inefficiency, without affecting the community. A deposit insurance scheme aims at sharing costs of bank failure only among participants of banking gains. It is a cost-selective device.

With these considerations in mind we can now examine the relation existing between Llr and deposit insurance.

With its unlimited resources and its discretionary power the Llr could keep the banking industry so sound that no bank would ever fail. No bank would leave the system because of its inefficiency. On the contrary, failures are an important source of market discipline and a public policy totally preventing runs is undesirable. What is desirable is to avoid that the effects of a widespread bank failure on the whole banking industry occur. An adequate operating deposit insurance ensures that insolvent banks can leave the industry without adversely affecting money shocks and economic activity.

If it is useful to identify the Llr's and deposit insurance's different goals, it is also important to consider some practical aspects arising from the co-existence of the two instruments.

Experience suggests that in the current institutional environment, where both inadequate deposit insurance funds and extensive performing Llr functions of central banks exist, the guarantees provided by these two devices supplement each other, moulding into a single public guarantee. In the case of a bankruptcy of a bank with a large amount of its liabilities, the insurance agency may be forced to borrow from the central bank to reimburse depositors. The insurance funds are often too small to cover major disturbances of the banking system and the implicit guarantee by the central bank to insurance scheme obligations is a necessary complement to it.

Moreover, the availability of emergency loans from the central bank acts as a substitute for deposit insurance reserves. It reduces the insurer's cost of maintaining a given set of deposit guarantee by creating a prime source of credit.

Because of this strict linkage with the lending facilities provided by the central bank, the value of the insurance guarantee often depends on the liquidity guarantees that the market expects the central bank to make available.[28] In this sense the central banks lending function makes it easier for the deposit insurance system to honour its commitments to insured depositors. But the Llr's intervention also provides another positive effect for the deposit insurers. It delays the need for the insurance funds to be utilised. Further time could be useful to manage a fair solution to the bank problems.

Thus, both the inadequacy of insurance funds and the practical benefits in terms of costs and timing which arise from the cooperation with Llr, make the existence of deposit insurance reduce but not eliminate the need for central bank lending in protecting the financial system.

Stressing the meaning of this it has been observed[29] that an effective and reliable Llr can also prevent runs from becoming dangerously widespread. Deposit insurance is considered as a regularising device for the payoff of depositors to the maximum possible extent from liquidations of the failed institutions. In this view deposit insurance is just a mechanism to settle claims from depositors quickly and it is not an essential to the safeguard of the financial system. If this were the real objective for establishing a deposit insurance scheme, this would be much more effective when structured as a trustee in bankruptcy since in that structure it is better at meeting the need for ensuring a bank winding up in the respect of the *par conditio creditorum*.

In our opinion deposit insurance is an instrument to be intended for handling bank failures in order to let banks work as competitive and efficient firms. Nevertheless, the particular nature of the insurance related to the particular structure and role of the insured institutions allows this instrument to affect depositors' expectations to eliminate the initial reason for bank runs and enforcing the public confidence in the system.

In this respect, deposit insurance has a specific rationale that, in spite of the existing interrelations and common objectives with Llr, makes it play a peculiar role in the system and justifies its presence together with the Llr.

NOTES

1. On this point see Calomiris and Gorton (1990).
2. See Bernanke (1983).
3. For example we omit the items relating to the federal funds market that transfers excess funds from small deposit-rich banks to large deposit-poor banks. These funds are a source of liquidity and are effective in facilitating the sharing of liquidity within the banks but including them in the balance sheet would not be useful for our reasoning. Furthermore in the balance sheet above we do not consider governmental securities. As bank portfolio items they do not raise any question in terms of information and valuation; they are immediately marketable and are not peculiar to bank investment activities and mostly they are financed using repurchase agreements and other sources of funds other than deposits.
4. Dyamond and Dybvig (1986).
5. Among others Ramakrishnam and Thaker (1984), Boyd and Prescott (1985).
6. The model considers entrepreneurs' projects where returns are independent.
7. Goodhart (1986) has focused on this point.
8. See Gorton (1989) and Gorton and Pennacchi (1990).
9. Asymmetric information arises from the fact that banks and depositors have not the same knowledge about the performance of bank management and portfolios.
10. See Chapter 2.
11. Calomiris and Gorton (1990) have provided an explicit definition of banking panics: "A banking panic occurs when bank debt holders at all, or many, banks in the banking system, suddenly demand that banks convert their debt into cash (at par) to such an extent that banks suspend convertibility of their debt into cash".
12. This definition is provided by Kaufman (1988), pg.562.
13. See Benston et al. (1986).
14. According to this definition of insolvency, total assets include loans and investments, off-balance sheets and contingent items, fee-based services, franchise value, benefits and any form of "goodwill" (Benston et al., 1986). This means that total assets include also intangible items which are not fully valued on the balance sheet.
15. On this point see Goodhart (1986).
16. On the concept of financial crises as externalities see Laassen (1985).
17. For a deeper analysis of Fdic see Chapter 5.
18. Coinsurance under the current system is practised with depositors who hold deposits in excess of $100.000 and with other creditors who hold unsecured

claims. The coinsurance aim is to share the risk between insurers and insured parties, in order to let the insurers participate in the risk. It is a device to induce depositors to monitor the banks' risk-taking behaviour.

19. The existing relation between deposit insurance and regulation is analysed in Chapter 3.

20. Differently from the Fdic the Fslic (Federal Savings and Loan Insurance Corporation) which is the U.S. government agency that provide deposit insurance for thrift institutions has experienced limits on the amount of its insurance coverage by requiring a minimum level of net worth.

21. See McCarthy (1980), Scott and Mayer (1971).

22. Merrick and Saunders (1985).

23. Carns (1989).

24. Merton (1989).

25. Goodhart (1986), (1987) and Goodman (1984).

26. See on this point Kanatas (1986).

27. Gibson (1972).

28. See Benston et al. (1986).

29. Schwartz (1987).

2 The rationale for deposit insurance

Deposit insurance is one of the possible institutional responses to banking system crises.

The rationale for this protection device is provided by the different theories on the origin of panics. By reflecting beliefs about the factors which contribute to the instability of the banking industry, each model leads to quite different conclusions about appropriate public policies towards bank and deposit insurance.

Competing theoretical models propose different views about the nature of banks, banking and panics. However, there is some common ground. In particular, all argue that the origin of panics is a change in that depositors' behaviour. Large deposit withdrawals, whatever their motivation, destroy the effectiveness of bank transformation services and cause interruptions in productive investments. Depositors' behaviour is therefore considered the key variable needed to explain bank system instability.

Nevertheless, recent developments in financial markets raise an additional issue to be explored in terms of stability in the banking industry.

The parallel growth of new and different types of financial transactions such as those involving interbank overnight funding, funding of bank final securities transfers and funding foreign exchange transactions, has required the creation of special provisional wire transfer networks. By participating in these networks, whilst increasing the volume of processed transfers, banks are susceptible to systemic risk. Because of the interbank relationships created by the payment system, the default of a large participant on its payment obligations could cause other participants to fall in a domino-like fashion.

Banks therefore are susceptible to instability because of the function they assume in the payment system. Widespread banking crises could be triggered by a single large institution failure as well as by a change in depositors' behaviour.

In this regard, historical experience provides an interesting example of market response to banking crises. During the nineteenth century, the US private clearinghouse associations were effective in mitigating the effects of panics by stressing their clearing function. When a panic occurred, clearinghouses operated to protect group soundness, by safeguarding the normal clearing process. By freeing currency they not only provided a form of insurance for deposits, but also provided a mechanism to ensure the settlement of obligations among participants.

2.1 DEPOSIT INSURANCE AND BANKING PANICS MODELS

The aim of preventing banking panics has always informed and rationalised government intervention into the banking industry. The establishment of deposit insurance systems in many different countries has constituted a response to this exigence. In particular, the choice of a deposit insurance scheme as a banking protection device represents a choice to share the peculiar risks of banking within the same banking system.

In practice, deposit insurance requires the government intervention as a complement to its activity. It involves growing economic and social costs that have to be compared with the benefit of banking stability in order to perceive whether the trade-off is favourable.

With this in view, recent literature has focused on the causes of banking panics, the performance of present instruments, and on the possibility of providing bank stability at a minimum cost. According to the different assumptions about the source of panics, economics literature provides different conclusions about the costs of panics and consequently provides different rationales for the devices that are considered effective in preventing banking instability.

The economic literature at issue provides two competitive approaches to bank panics and their causes, which by modelling different theoretical frameworks lead to different policy implications.

The first line of argument, initiated by the seminal work of Diamond and Dybvig (1983),[1] points out that bank runs are a "bad equilibrium"[2] of the banking system, in a model with two possible equilibria. The good equilibrium occurs where the optimal risk-sharing of the deposit contracts is achieved between different types of agents with different consumption needs; the bad equilibrium occurs where all agents panic and try to withdraw their deposit at the same time.

This theory, which is labelled non-fundamental,[3] asserts that bank runs are caused by "anything that causes (depositors) to anticipate a run" because of "a bad earnings report, a negative government forecast, or even a sunspot". Banking panics, therefore, are random manifestations of mob psychology or mass hysteria rooted in individual and collective behaviour. Because of this the theory is also described as "random withdrawal theory".[4] Events of an economic nature are not related to panics' causes, whereas the role of banks in providing transformation services matters. Banks are able to transform illiquid assets by offering liabilities with a different, smoother pattern of return over time than the illiquid assets offer. These contracts, which can be optimal if the confidence in the financial system is maintained, can force banks to liquidate illiquid assets with high social welfare costs if agents panic and incentives are distorted.

The model presents an explicit economic role for banks to perform, but, because of differing levels of confidence among agents, banks are at the same time vulnerable to runs. A multiple equilibria system exists according to the agents' behaviour.

The non-fundamental theory sees deposit insurance – governmental and not private – as a device effective in allowing demand deposit contracts to achieve the optimum equilibrium if an optimal tax is imposed to finance the insurance. The optimal tax allows the banks to follow a desirable asset liquidation policy that is exempt from cash-flow constraints imposed by deposit withdrawals. For all possible anticipated withdrawals, the optimal tax averts the participation in a bank run. Hence, a deposit insurance scheme, funded by optimal taxes, prevents runs.

33

In the random individual theory, deposit insurance is an effective instrument against panics because it makes the system a single equilibrium system, instead of a multi equilibria one.

The second type of theory advanced by the literature provides a fundamental framework for bank panics by arguing that they are systematically related to the occurrence of other events which changes perception of risk. Panics are seen as being caused by depositors' sudden and rational revision of the perceived risk of bank debt when they are uninformed about the value of the bank's asset portfolio and receive adverse news about the macroeconomy. Since depositors are unable to distinguish individual bank risks, if a signal gives them the perception of possible bank failures, they will withdraw a large volume of deposits from all banks, generating widespread runs.

This model assumes the existence of an information asymmetry between banks and depositors, that is, depositors are not able to assess accurately the risk of individual bank liabilities, and they may be forced to use non bank-specific aggregate information. In this environment, bank runs are viewed as serving a positive function in monitoring bank performance. Furthermore, bank runs occur as an unique equilibrium and they are triggered by rational revision in beliefs of banking performance.

Concerning the banks' role, the fundamental theory argues that banks provide valuable services through the creation of non marketable assets together with the provision of a medium of exchange. This theory differs from the previous one – banks do not exist to insure that consumption occurs in concert with the realisation of agents' consumption preferences – they exist to provide a medium of exchange. For that, the fundamental theory assumes the unit banking system as given and bank runs may be an optimal response of depositors to inherent bank weaknesses.

This line of argument has no single model as progenitor, but numerous researchers[5] have developed the argument for the asymmetric information-based view of banking panics. Many other authors have focused on the aggregate information which leads depositors to revise their perceived riskiness of banks, that is on the kind of "adverse news".

In this regard Gorton (1988) has pointed out that three versions of the fundamental theory exist. They assume different hypotheses on which variables change perceived risk, these are: seasonal hypothesis, failure hypothesis and recession hypothesis. The first views panics as caused by extreme seasonal fluctuations, the second views the unexpected failure of a typical financial institution as the immediate cause of panics, and finally the third focuses on recession as the origin of panics.

From the point of view of the fundamental theory, in each of its versions deposit insurance is considered an effective means whose availability guarantees the transformation of illiquid bank assets into cash. Deposit insurance in this environment is intended to maintain depositors' confidence in financial institutions even if bad news arrives. Thus deposit insurance assumes a meaning more in keeping with its insurance nature. Then, the fact that deposit insurance is effectively an insurance depends upon the structure and organization of the scheme. However, this instrument is far from the deposit insurance contemplated in the non-fundamental theory environment, where it serves an equilibrating function between two types of agents, those who want to withdraw their deposits early and those who want to do it later, preventing the latter from joining with the former, deserting their original incentive to a long term investment without a real substitutive incentive to consumption.

The deposit insurance scheme, as the non-fundamental theory outlines in its aim and structure (based on the optimal tax to finance the system), is far from the possibility of practical realization. The fundamental theory does not suggest a scheme for deposit insurance, pointing out only its role in preventing runs. Nevertheless by analysing the historical experience of banking panics during the U.S. National Banking Era, as many researchers[6] have done, it suggests the way towards a system founded on private bank coalitions.

As we shall see, the experience of clearinghouses systems during the pre Federal Reserve era was very successful in monitoring banks and mitigating the effects of panics by providing private insurance arrangements, and the present experience of some financial markets, such as the futures market, represents a response to the asymmetric information in terms of private co-insurance arrangements.[7] We shall come back to this argument, after the discussion of the analytical implications of the two competitive theories.

2.1.1 The non-fundamental theory of banking panics

The work of Bryant (1980) was the first to recognize the role of demand deposits in providing insurance against preference shocks. In his paper Bryant constructs a model[8] where deposit liabilities backed by risky assets are generated. The coexisting uninsurable demand for liquidity by individuals, that is, the uninsurable event of depositors withdrawing at any time, together with the asymmetric information on the risky assets give the financial intermediaries a signal – extraction problem. If a "bad outcome" occurs, individuals react by withdrawing their deposits, thus generating a bank run. A bank run is non-price rationing and it is a poor allocation scheme because it prevents the deposit contracts from being optimal with regard to the liquidity needs of individuals.

In this model, deposit insurance eliminates the non-price rationing which is inefficient and it is therefore useful even if does not necessarily prevent a bank run from occurring. But Bryant does not outline a scheme for deposit insurance. By considering the different devices government can employ to ensure deposits – a tax scheme, printing money, and redeeming bonds – he points out their different effectiveness, effects and costs but he identifies deposit insurance with government intervention in the banking system, independently from its technical forms. Diamond and Dybvig (1983) will develop that model, providing a scheme for deposit insurance.

The Diamond and Dybvig setting has three periods ($T = 0,1,2$) which could be referred to as the planning period ($T = 0$), the intermediate period ($T = 1$) and the final period ($T = 2$).[9] A single homogeneous good exists. The productive technology, which is the activity performed by banks, is riskless and yields $R > 1$ units of output in the final period for each unit of input in the planning period. If the production is interrupted in $T = 1$, the salvage value is just the initial investment.
The productive technology[10] is represented by the following returns:

$$
\begin{array}{ccc}
T = 0 & T = 1 & T = 2 \\
-1 & \left\{ \begin{array}{c} 0 \\ 1 \end{array} \right. & \left\{ \begin{array}{c} 2 \\ 0 \end{array} \right.
\end{array}
$$

where in the intermediate period the choice between $(0,R)$ and $(0,1)$ is made by choosing to interrupt the production at $T = 1$ or to let it work up to $T = 2$. In the former case the return is 1 at $T = 1$ and 0 at $T = 2$, in the latter case the return is 0 at $T = 1$ and R at $T = 2$. The technology considered supposes long-term capital investments which, if liquidated before maturity, involves high transaction costs.

Consumers in this model are N and are of two kinds: type 1, impatient consumers and type 2, patient.[11] At $T = 0$ they are all identical and each faces a privately observed uninsurable risk of becoming type 1 or type 2 agents. Impatient agents care only about consumption in $T = 1$, which means that they interrupt the production at $T = 1$, earning a return of 1. Patient agents on the contrary care only about consumption in $T = 2$. They will interrupt the production at $T = 2$.

In this model the optimal equilibrium is achieved when

$$r_1 = c_1^{1*} \tag{1}$$

where r_1 = fixed payment for unit deposited at $T = 0$ and withdrawn at $T = 1$;

C_1^{1*} = optimal consumption of impatient agent.

This equilibrium achieves optimal risk sharing among agents who need to consume at different times given full information. Equation (1) represents a contract which secures an equilibrium for the impatient to withdraw at $T = 1$, and for the patient to wait, without any alteration in the self-selection[12] of agents between impatient and patient.

If, on the contrary, the optimal contract is in place and a sunspot induces all agents to panic and to withdraw at $T = 1$ the equilibrium inherent in equation (1) becomes a bad equilibrium. All agents deny their self-selection, based on their consumption need, by all becoming type 1. A run occurs that ruins the risk sharing between agents and reduces the efficiency of production because all production is interrupted at the intermediate period ($T = 1$) when it is optimal for some to continue until the final one ($T = 2$).

Equation (1) represents the existing relationship between optimal consumption and the demand deposit contract. Let us return to each of these concepts following Diamond and Dybvig's reasoning.

In their model, each agent has a state-dependent utility function which is assumed to have the form:

$$U(C_1, C_2; \Theta) = \begin{cases} (C_1) & \text{if } j \text{ is of type 1 in state} \\ \\ (C_1 + C_2) & \text{if } j \text{ is of type 2 in state} \end{cases}$$

Let C_T represent the consumption by an agent at period T. Thus C_1 is the consumption at $T = 1$, and $C_1 + C_2$ is the consumption at $T = 2$ by agent of type 2, because he could obtain consumption goods at $T = 1$ and he can privately store then until $T = 2$ to consume them. Then the privately observed consumption at $T = 2$ of the patient agent is what he stores or hoards from $T = 1$ plus what he obtains at $T = 2$. Θ represents the state, ρ is $1 \geq \rho R^{-1}$ and μ: $R_{++} \to R$ is twice continuously differentiable, increasing, strictly concave and satisfies Inada conditions $\mu'(0) = \infty$ and $\mu'(\infty) = 0$. The utility function displays relative risk aversion greater than unity, that is $-C\mu''(C)/\mu'(C) > 1$. The objective of agents is to maximize the expected utility of consumption:

$$\text{Max } E \left[\mu(C_1, C_2; \Theta) \right]$$

eventually conditional on their information.

The fraction of the population (N) which is type 1 is, for the moment, a constant $t \in (0,1)$, and each agent as an equal independent chance of being of type 1. Finally, each agent has endowed with one unit of the planning period good.

Diamond and Dybving demonstrate that in the simple contingent-claims market, where agents hold their assets directly, there is room to improve the outcome. That is, an insurance arrangement might be preferred to a competitive solution because agents are willing to forgo some of their consumption if they turn out to be patient, in return for a greater consumption if they turn out to be impatient. It means that the optimal insurance contract would allow agents to insure against the unlucky outcome of being type 1 agents.

In fact, in the competitive solution, there is a competitive market in claims on future goods in each time period. Given the identical position of each agent at $T = 0$, there will be a trade in claims on food for consumption at $T = 1$ and $T = 2$. Each consumer has access to the same technology and each can choose any positive linear combination of both $C_1 = 1$ and $C_2 = R$. Given C_k^i, the consumption in period k of an agent of type 1, the agents choose $C_1^1 = 1, C_2^1 = C_1^2 = 0$ and $C_2^2 = R$, since agents of type 1 always interrupt production and type 2 never do.

On the contrary, if agents pool their resources in an insurance arrangement it would be possible to unite optimal insurance contracts that give the optimal sharing of output between type 1 and type 2 agents. The optimal consumption $\{C_k^{i*}\}$ satisfies:

$$C_1^{2*} = C_2^{1*} = 0 \tag{2a}$$

$$\mu'(C_1^{2*}) = \rho R \mu'(C_2^{2*}) \tag{2b}$$

$$tC_1^{1*} + [(1 - t)C_2^{2*}/R] = 1 \tag{2c}$$

where (2a) signifies that those who can, delay consumption, (2b) indicates that marginal utility is in line with marginal productivity, and (2c) is the resource constraint. Condition (2c) could be written as

$$(1 - t)C_2^{2*} = R(1 = tC_1^{1*})$$

where the term in parentheses on the right is what is left over in period $T = 1$ after the impatient agents are paid off. Because of the assumption of $R > 1$, and since relative risk aversion exceeds unity, equation (2) implies that the optimal consumption levels satisfy $C_1^{1*} > 1$ and $C_2^{2*} < R$, and $C_2^{2*} > C_1^{1*}$. The competitive outcome, as we have seen, implies $C_1^1 = 1$ and $C_2^2 = R$. The optimal insurance contract, thus, satisfies the self-selection constraints.

Diamond and Dybvig argue that banks can provide this insurance. Banks, in fact, guarantee a reasonable return when the agent cashes in before maturity, as is required for optimal risk-sharing. At this point, the demand deposit contract has to be settled.

The model gives each agent who withdraws at $T = 1$ a fixed claim of r_1 per unit deposited at $T = 0$. The model also assumes that the first come first served rule will work. It means that withdrawals are served sequentially in random order until the bank runs out of assets. The payoff by the bank to any agent depends only on the agent's place in the line and not on future information about agents behind him in the line.

Furthermore the model assumes that the bank is mutually owned and liquidated at $T = 2$, so that agents not withdrawing at $T = 1$ get a pro rata share of the bank's assets in $T = 2$.

39

We can now define V_1 and V_2, respectively, the payoff at $T = 1$ per unit deposit withdrawn, which depends on agent's place in line at $T = 1$, and the $T = 2$ payoff per unit deposit not withdrawn at $T = 2$, which depends on total withdrawals at $T = 1$. These are

$$V_1(f_j, r_1) = \begin{cases} r_1 & \text{if } f_j < r_1^{-1} \\ 0 & \text{if } f_j \ge r_1^{-2} \end{cases} \qquad (3)$$

and

$$V_2(f, r_2) = \max \{R(1 - r_1 f)/1 - f), 0\} \qquad (4)$$

where $\quad f_j \quad = \quad$ number of withdrawers's deposits received before agent j as a fraction of total demand deposits;

$\quad f \quad = \quad$ total number of demand deposits withdrawn.

Now, this demand deposit contract achieves full information optimal risk sharing when $r_1 = C_1^{1*}$, as we have seen, that is when the fixed payment per dollar of deposits withdrawn at the intermediate period is equal to the optimal consumption of patient agents given full information.

As Diamond and Dybving point out it is precisely the transformation of illiquid assets into liquid liabilities that is responsible both for the liquidity service provided by banks and for their susceptibility to runs. In fact, looking at the value of r_1, if it is equal to C_1^{1*} the good equilibrium is achieved; if, $r_1 > 1$ runs are a probability, and if $r_1 = 1$ a bank would not be susceptible to runs. This occurs because $V_1(f_j, 1) < V_2(f, 1)$ for all values of $0 \le f_j \le f$, but, at the same time, there is no improvement on a simple competitive claims market, as, on the contrary a demand deposit contract is able to provide. In this case, when $r_1 = 1$, bank simply mimics direct holding of the assets. The value $r_1 = 1$, is the value which rules out runs and mimics the competitive market because it is the per unit intermediate period liquidating value of the technology. Thus a demand deposit contract which is not subject to runs provides no liquidity services.

The model provides a rationale for banks' intermediation services and for banks' runs simultaneously. It implies that the unique role of banks is founded on a very fragile equilibrium and that banks are very concerned about maintaining confidence. The next step in Diamond and Dybvig's reasoning is to develop a variation of the demand deposit contract which will protects banks, depositors and the system against runs. The two possible variations are: suspension of convertibility, that is suspension of allowing the withdrawal of deposits, and deposit insurance. The authors argue that the latter devices are provided by governments and can produce superior contracts.

If the suspension of convertibility is in use, impatient people would still show up in the intermediate period for their withdrawals, but the patient consumers' incentive to withdraw early is eventually removed, and the phenomenon of bank panics can not possibly occur.

The contract is identical to the pure demand deposit contract (equations (3) and (4)), but it states that any agent will receive nothing at $T = 1$ if he attempts to withdraw at $T = 1$ after a fraction $\hat{f} < r_1^{-1}$ of all deposits have already been withdrawn. The contract is now:

$$V_1^s(f_j, r_1) = \begin{cases} r_1 & \text{if } f_j \leq \hat{f} \\ 0 & \text{if } f_j > \hat{f} \end{cases}$$

$$V_1^s(f_j, r_1) = \max \left\{ \frac{(1 - fr_1)R}{1 - f}, \frac{(1 - \hat{f}r_1)R}{1 - \hat{f}} \right\}$$

where, $1 - \hat{f}r_1$ is assumed to be greater than zero.

When, $f_j = \hat{f}$ then convertibility of deposits to cash is suspended and anyone else who shows up in period $T = 1$ is allowed to withdraw. If this contract is working, type 2 agents are ensured to satisfy their consumption needs at $T = 2$, and any early withdrawals at $T = 1$ would be costly compared with the period 2 withdrawals. That is for all f and $f_j \leq f$, $V_2^s > V_f^s$.

If $r_1 = C_1^{1*}$ and $\hat{f} \in t, [(R - r_1)/r_1(R - 1)]$, the contract can achieve the optimal allocation. All impatient agents will withdraw everything at $T = 1$, because period 2 consumption is worthless for them, and all patient agents will wait until $T = 2$ to withdraw.

The contract is very stable and there is a unique Nash equilibrium that achieves optimal risk-sharing. Even if some agents are irrational other agents will choose their equilibrium actions. The suspension of convertibility guarantees that it will never be profitable to participate in a bank run. However the suspension of convertibility contracts works perfectly only if t is known and not stochastic. If t is constant, as we have supposed till now, $\hat{f}$ is determined. On the other hand, if t is an unobserved random variable, that is, it is not possible to identity ex ante the fraction of N which are impatient, $f_j = \hat{f}$, as a condition for suspension is not determined. The suspension of convertibility contracts achieves optimal risk sharing when t is known ex ante because suspension never occurs in equilibrium and the bank can provide the optimal asset liquidation policy. When t is random it can be demonstrated that no bank contract, including suspension of convertibility, can achieve the full information optimum. On the other hand deposit insurance is shown to be able to rule out runs without reducing the ability of banks to transform assets.

In the Diamond and Dybvig model, deposit insurance provides a real service by separating the desirable asset liquidation policy of banks from the cash-flow constraint imposed directly by withdrawals. Deposit insurance prevents runs to the extent that an optimal tax is imposed ex-post on agents' proceeds from their withdrawals. The crucial point for an effective deposit system is its ability in imposing such a tax. The reason for this is that deposit insurance is viewed as a device provided by government; only the government, in fact, has the authority to levy taxes at a fair level. Government intervention then realises an ex-post taxation of those agents who withdraw early in period $T = 1$. In this environment for all possible anticipated withdrawals of other agents, it never pays to participate in a bank run and confidence in the system is preserved.

Thus, it is fundamental to identify the optimal tax that allows demand deposit contracts to achieve the unconstrained optimum as a unique Nash equilibrium. The optimal tax prevents the bad equilibrium from occurring, but allows, on the other hand, demand deposit contracts to achieve the good equilibrium. That is, tax-financed deposit insurance is able to duplicate the optimal consumption $C_1^1(t) = C_1^{1*}(t)$, $C_2^2(t) = C_2^{2*}(t)$, $C_2^1(t) = 0$ and $C_1^2(t) = 0$ from the optimal risk sharing characterized in equation (2).

In the Diamond and Dybving model the government is supposed to impose a tax on all wealth at the beginning of the intermediate period ($T = 1$). This tax is payable either in goods or in deposits. Let deposits be accepted for taxes at the pre-tax amount of good which could be obtained if withdrawn at $T = 1$. The amount of tax that must be raised in the intermediate period depends on the number of withdrawals, f, and the asset liquidation policy. The tax $\tau(f)$ is given by:

$$\tau(f) = \begin{cases} 1 - \dfrac{c_1^{1*}(f)}{r_1} & \text{if } f \le \bar{t} \\[2mm] 1 - r_1^{-1} & \text{if } f > \bar{t} \end{cases}$$

where $\bar{t}$ is the greatest possible realization of , that is, of t as a random variable.

The after-tax proceeds, per unit of initial deposit of withdrawal at $T = 1$ depends on f through the tax payment and is identical for all $f_j \le f$. The after-tax proceeds are given by:

$$\hat{V}_1(f) = \begin{cases} c_1^{1*}(f) & \text{if } f \le \bar{t} \\[2mm] 1 & \text{if } f > \bar{t} \end{cases}$$

The after-tax proceeds, per unit of initial deposit, of a withdrawal at $T = 2$ are determined by the net payments[13] to the impatient agents , thus

$$\hat{V}_2(f) = \begin{cases} \dfrac{R\{1 - [c_1^{1*}(f)f]\}}{1-f} = c_2^{2*}(f) & \text{if } f \le \bar{t} \\[3mm] \dfrac{R(1-f)}{1-f} = R & \text{if } f > \bar{t} \end{cases}$$

for all $f \in [0,1]$, $\hat{V}_1(f) < \hat{V}_2(f)$, and $\hat{V}_1(f) > 0$.

It implies that no patient agents will withdraw at $T = 1$, even if they expect offers to withdraw, and all impatient agents will withdraw at $T = 1$. Therefore, the unique dominant strategy equilibrium is $f = t$, the realization of t. If evaluated at a realization $\bar{t}$, $\hat{V}_1(f)$ and $\hat{V}_2(f)$ become

$$\hat{V}_1(f = t) = c_1^{1*}(t)$$

and

$$\hat{V}_2(f = t) = \frac{[1 - tc_1^1(t)]R}{1-t} = c_2^{2*}(t)$$

that is, the optimal consumption and risk sharing characterized in equation (2).

43

The model implies that government will follow an unconstrained tax policy. But if t is random and a non-optimal tax is imposed there will be some distortion and costs associated with government deposit insurance, such that social welfare could be higher without the insurance.

The model, then, focuses on the role of government policy in providing deposit insurance as a device to prevent a bad equilibrium, rather than a policy to move an already existing equilibrium.

Diamond and Dybvig's work focuses on the role banks are performing by transforming illiquid assets into liquid liabilities and the foundations of banks' vulnerability to runs and on the nature of deposit contracts they provide.

Demand deposits issued by banks can improve on a competitive market by providing, as we have seen, better risk sharing among people who have different consumption needs at different random times. Banks, then, provide insurance against preference shocks. But demand deposit contracts have an undesirable equilibrium, where exogenous variables can induce depositors to panic, even those who would prefer to leave their deposits if they were not concerned about the bank failing. Thus, the unique role of intermediation provided by banks is the rationale for both their existence and for their susceptibility to runs.

Banks runs are costly in terms of social welfare. If a bank fails, it has to recall loans. This has two negative kinds of effects: it interrupts productive investment and destroys optimal risk sharing among depositors. Furthermore if runs occur in many banks, economy-wide problems could arise together with the disruption of the monetary system. In preventing the demand deposit contract from incurring a "bad equilibrium", deposit insurance is the most effective device. It allows bank contracts to achieve their optimality and eliminates the incentive for bank runs. A shift in depositors' expectations in the presence of deposit insurance does not give rise to runs. Depositors have no incentives to withdraw at different times with respect to their consumption preferences.

The model outlines an insurance system operating as an ex-post taxation on depositors' proceeds and it is based on the optimality of this taxation. The optimality of the taxation is not viewed in terms of pricing the insurance, but rather in terms of the real service it can provide by letting banks pursue asset liquidation policies more independently from the volume of withdrawals.

The "tax" is structured as a wealth transfer from the impatient to the patient agents, or vice-versa, so that the ex-ante optimal risk sharing is achieved, letting only the impatient withdraw at $T = 1$.

The assumption of a riskless technology is essential to the model and it represents, at the same time, its limit. If the technology is risky, then the choice of bank loan portfolio matters and any device introduced in the banking system has to be considered in relation to its effects on banks' risk-taking.

For this reason different models of non-fundamental theory have been developed with both the objectives. It is necessary to reconsider the constraint imposed by the riskless technology assumption and to make clear what type of events would cause beliefs to change such that a panic would occur.

One of the main contributions concerning the analysis of deposit insurance costs, in terms of distortions of bank decisions (moral hazard), and in terms of causes of panics, is by Chari (1989).

Chari models a framework very close to Diamond and Dybvig's within which he makes it possible to evaluate the effectiveness of alternative policies in preventing panics. The conclusions he draws are, however, very different from Diamond and Dybving's, especially in that he argues deposit insurance is not the only effective arrangement in forestalling bank panics.

By observing the historical experience of banking panics, in such similar economies as the United States, Great Britain and Canada, Chari argues that the former experienced panics during the 19th and early 20th centuries, unlike the latter, due to the different institutional arrangements of the banking systems. The United States banking system was prohibited from branching between and within States, and banks were permitted to meet their reserve requirements partly by deposits at national banks in designated reserve cities, whereas Great Britain and Canada did not introduce this regulation. As a result, the United States system was subject to community specific variations in the demand for currency and it could not diversify this risk by issuing deposits directly in other communities. On the other hand, permitting reserves to be held as deposits in other banks caused these banks to operate with a more illiquid portfolio. Thus, the system, on the whole, was particularly susceptible to bank panics.

In this framework Chari recognizes in banks' failure to diversify

45

withdrawal risk the main characteristic that makes them vulnerable to runs.

In developing his reasoning Chari uses some modified versions of Diamond and Dybvig and Wallace (1988) models. The resulting model provides a useful framework to analyse a system where withdrawals are random and aggregate risk therefore exists, and it is able to capture the key features of U.S. National Banking system as described above.

In this model, as Chari shows, bank panics are possible and suspension of convertibility does not eliminate them entirely. Bank panics are still triggered by shifts in agents' beliefs concerning other agents' behaviour, and they are costly because they distort consumption decisions away from the desirable outcome.

Chari's original contribution to the non-fundamental theory of bank panics is in the development of this model by considering the possibility that demand for currency can vary within communities, rather than within a unit system.

Let us suppose that there are a large number of communities and that each has N people – The fraction of impatient people in each community can be t_1 and t_2, where $t_2 > t_1$ with probability p_1 and p_2 respectively. Each community replicates the aggregate-risk economy. Because there are a large number of communities, the aggregate economy does not have random withdrawal. Impatient agents in the economy wide population are $t = p_1 t_1 + p_2 t_2$.

If the communities could pool their resources, their collective economy would look exactly like the Diamond and Dybvig model. In the Chari model, communities are assumed to be isolated. This means that at $T = 0$ each community has its specific good that cannot be transported elsewhere, unlike period $T = 1$ and $T = 2$ when it is possible. Information does not circulate across communities, so the realization of the fraction of type 1 agents is not observable across communities. In the intermediate and final period communities can borrow and lend from each other. If a liquid technology is introduced in the model, that is, a technology which produces one unit of output in the next period from one unit of investment in the current period, then the model is not susceptible to runs.

Each community is supposed to invest an amount $t_1 x_1$ (per capita) of resources in the liquid technology[14], and each community promises to pay x_1 units to those who withdraw at $T = 1$ and x_2 units to those who

46

remain in the final period.[15] Furthermore all economies can borrow and lend at $T = 1$ at an interest rate $x_2/x_1 > 1$.[16]

Any community which faces the t_2 fraction of type 1 agents pays off the first t impatient agents from liquid technology (reserves) and borrows $(t_2 - t)x_1$ in the market to pay off the remaining patient agents. In the final period these communities pay x_2 units to each of their $(1 - t_2)$ patient agents and $(t_2 - t)x_2$ to their lenders. In the same way communities facing t_1 type 1 agents could be viewed lending at $T = 1$ their remaining reserves after the payoff of the impatient agents. In this framework, single community swings in the desired amount of currency could be observed by other communities, reducing the risk for an economy wide risk of panic.

Thus if an interbank borrowing and lending market is well-functioning within the banking system, then the incentive to runs arising from local shocks is prevented. In this environment banks could self-insure by moving reserves about through the interbank loan market. In this model the central bank's discount window, rather than deposit insurance, can play a key role in preventing bank panics.

The central bank, in fact can work by holding total reserves of other banks and lending at the gross interest rate of x_2/x_1 against assets that have a longer maturity period. This interest rate is higher than the return on reserves (unity) and lower than the rate of return on the assets (R). By allowing such below-market borrowing, the central bank can provide an important insurance role. As Chari points out, the premium for this insurance contract is paid in the form of reserves held at the central bank.

The mechanism for lending by the central bank in Chari's model does not generate moral hazard problems for banks. The lending is done against sound assets, and depositors, who are uninsured, are interesting in monitoring bank risk-taking.

On the other hand, deposit insurance, because of its moral hazard implication, needs external monitoring by regulation.

Thus, as we have seen, two different versions of the same theory that of Diamond and Dybvig and that of Chari, have very distinctive policy implications concerning the stability of the financial system.

Regardless of their differences, the two models are complementary to the extent that the second provides an explanation of what causes panics other than "sunspots". By identifying the seasonality of the demand for currency as the panic causing shocks, the second model we have analysed contributes to theoretical development of the non-fundamental theory. Nevertheless this theoretical framework is built on the capacity of banks to provide a unique intermediary service by insuring that agents' consumption preference is satisfied. Any policy intervention is viewed as a guarantee for the banking system to provide, without constraints, optimal contracts and then to provide liquidity to the system as intertemporal consumption flexibility[17], in spite of the illiquidity of assets.

2.1.2 The fundamental theory of banking panics

The second line of argument in the origin of panics represents an alternative theory in that it is based on identifying the conditions under which depositors would rationally change their beliefs about the riskiness of banks.

In the fundamental framework for bank panics, sunspots are not of concern. Some other economic events are responsible for the rational revision of agents' perceived risk of bank debt, and for runs or system-wide panics. The common feature of models developing this theory is the hypothesis about the incomplete information about the value of banks assets. It means that, given the asymmetry of information between banks and depositors, depositors cannot costlessly value individual banks' assets; if depositors change, on a rational basis, their perception of asset riskiness they will not be able to discern which bank is under-performing. They will be induced to withdraw from the banking system as a whole, leading the system into panic.

The models of Chari and Jagannathan (1984) and of Jacklin and Bhattacharya (1988), have clearly pointed out the role of information in generating panic events in the banking system.

Chari and Jagannathan model a framework where some individuals withdraw because they get information that future returns are likely to be low. Uninformed individuals observing this also have an incentive to liquidate their investment. Furthermore, some individuals withdraw deposits for reasons which are not informationally based. Thus, if the random realization of such a group of individuals is unusually large, then the uninformed individual will be misled and will participate in a run on the bank.

Asymmetric information and a sequential service constraint are

48

essential to this model in providing a rationale for bank panics as they are in the Jacklin and Bhattacharya framework. In their view, the role of private information about bank loan/asset pay-offs as the source of runs, is emphasized.

Furthermore the work of Jacklin and Bhattacharya was explicitly aimed at contrasting the conceptual and regulatory issues relating to intermediation, in particular to contrast with the Diamond and Dybvig model (1983). Their model outlines an economy where bank runs are information-based, depositors have smooth preferences and the underlying assets of the bank are risky. The model is characterized by two sources of asymmetric information: the bank cannot observe the true liquidity needs of depositors, and depositors are asymmetrically informed about the quality of the bank's assets. In this environment bank runs occur as a unique equilibrium when some depositors get bad news about the return on the risky assets.

In 1988, a paper by Gorton provided a fundamental theory model where asymmetric information, depositors' rational behaviour and a particular kind of "bad news" are put together to explain banking panics. The model uses empirical evidence arising from some tests of different monetary regimes in the U.S.

The central idea of Gorton is that, as panics are triggered by depositors' response to the occurrence of a threshold value of economic variables predicting the riskiness of bank deposits, panics can be explained by economic theory explaining consumer behaviour during non-panic times.

Thus, a theoretical framework is provided to describe the behaviour of the deposit-currency ratio and then some tests are carried out to study whether this description explains depositor behaviour at panic dates. The hypothesis is that when consumers forecast a coming recession because a variable predicting a recession reaches a critical level, they withdraw deposits in advance to avoid losses due to bank failures. In particular, the Gorton setting focuses on liabilities of failed business as the important variable predicting recession and then causing banking panics.

This analysis confirms that there is something special about panics, but in a very different way from random withdrawal theories. The special event is not a sunspot, rather it is the information that something special to the economy is about to happen.

Gorton's model of deposit-currency ratio is built on a Baumol-Tobin economy: consumption goods are purchased with currency and transactions within banks are costly. The number of transactions are m_t, X_t is the real consumption and p_t the price level.

Currency (C) and deposit holdings (D) during period t are defined as:[18]

$$C_t \equiv X_t \left(\frac{1}{m_t} \right) p_t;$$

$$D_t \equiv X_t \left(1 - \frac{1}{m_t} \right) p_t;$$

and their average values are:

$$\overline{C}_t = \left(\frac{1}{2} \right) C_t;$$

$$\overline{D}_t = \left(\frac{1}{2} \right) D_t;$$

Current consumption and transactions are financed by last period's savings and income. Thus the objective of the representative consumer is to maximize the following utility function:

$$MAX: E_t \left\{ \sum_{1-t} \beta^{1-t} U(X_i) | I_t \right\} \tag{1}$$
$$m_t$$

subject to the budget constrain :

$$x_t + \alpha m_t \leq (1 - r_{\alpha t-1} - \pi_{t-1}) \frac{\overline{D}_{t-1}}{p_t} + y_{t-1}$$

where the budget constraint requires that consumption and current transactions costs $(X_t + \alpha m_t)$, be financed by income carried at $t - 1(Y_{t-1})$ and by the return on savings (terms on the right side), held at $t - 1$. In expression (1) are:

$$\beta = \text{subjective rate of time preference;}$$

β = subjective rate of time preference;
I_t = information set available at time t;
α = real cost of a transaction;
r_{dt-1} = real rate of return ex-ante on average balance deposit money unit held during $t-1$;
π_{t-1} = real capital loss on average balance deposit monetary unit;
Y_{t-1} = real income at $t-1$

The first order condition for problem (1) is:

$$\alpha U'_t = E_t \left\{ \beta U' x_{t+1}(1 + r_{dt} - \pi_t) \left(\frac{1}{2}\right)(X_t)\left(\frac{1}{2}\right)^2 | I_t \right\} \qquad \text{(a)}$$

which is a stochastic Euler equation. Solving for m_t, the deposit-currency ratio is obtained:

$$\left[\frac{\overline{D}_t}{\overline{C}_t} + 1\right]^2 = E_t \left\{ \beta \left(\frac{X_{t+1}}{X_t}\right)^{-A} \frac{\left(\frac{1}{2}\right) X_t}{\alpha} (1 + r_{dt} - \pi_t) | I_t \right\} \qquad \text{(b)}$$

where A is the coefficient of relative aversion, assumed constant in the utility function.
    By letting

$$S_t \equiv \beta \left(\frac{X_{t+1}}{X_t}\right)^{-A} \frac{\left(\frac{1}{2}\right) X_t}{\alpha}$$

the (b) can be expressed as:

$$\left[\frac{\overline{D}_t}{\overline{C}_t} + 1\right]^2 = E_t \{S_t | I_t\} E_t \{(1 + r_{dt} - \pi_t) | I_t\} + \qquad \text{(c)}$$

$$+ \; Cov \; (S_t \; ; \; (1 + r_{dt} - \pi_t) | I_t)$$

This equation is the basic description of the deposit currency ratio, that is the liquidity function for the consumer studied by Gorton. This model of consumer behaviour assumes the banking system as given, which is very different from Diamond and Dybving's model where a rationale for an optimal deposit contract is provided. In that model deposit contracts play the role of an insurance against unobservable depositor consumption preferences. Here, deposits are securities provided by banks and are viewed in relation to currency.

Equation (c) describes the deposit-currency ratio as a function of expectations about the rate of return on demand deposits, the intertemporal terms of trade (S_t), and the covariance between the two. The covariance in (c) is not time invariant and it depends on the depositor's information.

The analysis of (c) is aimed at determining the information which affects the expected rate of return and the covariance to such a point that the deposit-currency ratio declines, causing a panic. The model does not explain panics; it is useful to identify, through empirical estimates, which variables have the capacity to trigger panics by moving to "special" values.

To estimate the model, a different version of it is needed. By adopting an "empirical strategy", the testable version of (c) proposed by Gorton is:

$$\left[\frac{\overline{D}_t}{\overline{C}_t} + 1 \right] = \alpha_0 + \alpha_1 t + \alpha_2 t^2 + \alpha_3 (1 + r_{dt} - \pi_t^2) + \quad (d)$$

$$+ \alpha_0 \, Cov_t^e + \mu_1$$

$$\alpha_3 = EXP \, [\beta_1 ln(X_{t+1}/X_t) + \beta_2 ln X_t]$$

$$\pi_t = \begin{cases} Z_t \tau + \varepsilon_t & \text{if } Z_t \tau + \varepsilon_t > 0 \\ 0 & \text{if } Z_t \tau + \varepsilon_t \leq 0 \end{cases} \quad (e)$$

$$Cov \equiv (X_{t+1} - X_t)\pi_t = \begin{cases} Z_t \tau + \varepsilon_t & \text{if } Z_t \tau + \varepsilon_t > 0 \\ 0 & \text{if } Z_t \tau + \varepsilon_t \leq 0 \end{cases} \quad (f)$$

This version has some particular features.

The total expected rate of return on demand deposits consists of two components (r_{dt}) and (π_t^e), where the first is contractually agreed upon by banks and depositors ex-ante so that it is known at time t, the second is expected capital loss; the capital loss (π_t) is constrained to be positive or zero, because demand deposits never earn capital gains.[19] Z_t is a matrix of predictors of capital costs. Cov_t^e, namely the estimated value of covariance in the t period is the perceived risk. As Gorton shows, the expected covariance indicates the depositor's conditional forecast of how consumption and losses on deposits will co-vary. Finally, from equation (f) it is plain that only a part of covariance is forecasted namely the expected product of the change in consumption, and the capital loss. W_t is a matrix of predictors.

The model described in (d) (e) and (f)[20] has been used to test different hypotheses over different banking eras in the United States, in order to capture different institutional conditions under which panics occurred. The first period examined is the National Banking Era (1865-1916). In this period neither the Federal Reserve System nor the Fdic were operating, two fundamental institutions that may be expected to affect depositors' behaviour. For that reason the National Banking period is considered the most significant for purposes of investigating panics and the estimates from that era are reference points in analysing subsequent periods. The other periods analysed are characterized by the introduction of the Fed in 1914 and by the establishment of the Fdic in 1934.

For the tests during the National Banking Era an empirical strategy was needed, because of a lack of data.[21] Nevertheless, the estimates are significant.

The three crucial hypotheses tested on the model (d) (e) and (f) are: the systematicity of panics, their predictability and the most plausible content of the information set with variables capturing seasonal effects, failures or recession.

The test results are the following. First, nothing happens at panic dates which cannot being explained by the model, that is, panics could be described as systematic events. Second, panics are predictable on the basis of prior information. Finally, panics tend to correspond to the largest values of the liabilities shocks of failed businesses. This means that panics are systematic events linked to the business cycle.

In terms of the model – equation (d) – panics are systematic events because the inclusion of a dummy variable for panic dates does not affect the model. It is not significant. On the contrary, if it had been significant it would have meant that panics are caused by extraneous events, like sunspots.

Panics are predictable because the perceived risk variable is significant. In particular it is significant where contemporaneous predictors are omitted in the extricating of equation (f), that is, the predictor of Cov_t does not include contemporaneous information. Hence, if on the basis of prior information, Cov_t^e is negative, then depositors shift from deposits to currency in order to avoid capital losses they expect to occur.

Finally, the liabilities of failed business variables are always significant as predictors of panics. At every panic date they achieve a critical value that they do not achieve on other dates. Banks hold claims on firms, and when firms begin to fail in sufficiently large members, it signals the onset of recession. Panics are likely to occur, because depositors reassess the riskiness of deposits. Table 2.1 shows the existing relationships among the business cycle peaks, the occurrence of panics, the increase of the currency-deposit ratio, and the decline in output as measured by a proxy, pig iron production. The losses to depositors and the percentage of national bank failures are also displayed. Bank panics, according with the table, tended to occur just after business cycle peaks.

Table 2.1: National banking era panics

Cycle Peak-Trough	Panic Date	% Δ (C/D)[1]	% Pig[2] Iron	Loss per deposit ($)	% of national bank failures
Oct. 1873-Mar. 1879	Sept. 1873	14.5	−51.0	0.021	2.8
Mar. 1882-May 1885	Jun. 1884	8.8	−14.0	0.008	0.9
Mar. 1887-Apr. 1888	No Panic	3.0	−9.0	0.005	0.4
Jul. 1890-May1891	Nov. 1890	9.0	−34.0	0.001	0.4
Jan. 1893-Jun. 1894	May 1893	16.0	−29.0	0.017	1.9
Dec. 1895-Jun. 1897	Oct. 1896	14.3	−4.0	0.012	1.6
Jun. 1899-Dec. 1900	No Panic	2.8	−6.7	0.001	0.3
Sep. 1902-Aug. 1904	No Panic	−4.1	−8.7	0.001	0.6
May 1907–Jun. 1902	Oct. 1907	11.4	−46.5	0.001	0.3
Jan. 1910-Jan. 1912	No Panic	−2.6	−21.7	0.0002	0.1
Jan. 1913-Dec. 1914	Aug. 1914	10.4	−47.1	0.001	0.4

1. Percentage change of currency/deposit ratio
2. Percentage change in pig iron production measured from peat to trough

Source: Gorton (1988)

The estimating of the model over other two periods, the Fed and Fdic period, demonstrates that the two institutional modifications in the monetary regime affected the behaviour of depositors, by altering their perception of risk.

After 1914, both the perceived risk and deposit currency ratio equations exhibit significant changes. In particular, the examined timing relations between liabilities, shocks and panics, when compared to the same timing relations during the National Banking Era, show that the introduction of the Federal Reserve system shifted the timing of panics, by changing depositors' behaviour. However, it was not able to prevent panics. The crisis of the '30s is the most evident example.

In the same way, the establishment of Fdic in 1934 altered depositors' behaviour. Nevertheless, this institutional reform was effective in preventing panics. In fact, several cases of large failed business liabilities shocks occurred after 1934, but none of them precipitated panics.

The estimating of the Gorton model over the period 1935-1972 shows the success of deposit insurance. In fact, expecting to consume more income during recessions, depositors increased their deposit-currency ratios. The model, therefore, provides a rationale for deposit insurance, founded on the empirical relevance of its effectiveness in preventing panic. In particular according to the logic of the model, the presence of deposit insurance in the banking system, attenuates the change in depositors' behaviour by making the deposit-currency ratio less responsive to negative signals about the outlook of the real economy. Deposit insurance reduces the incentive to collect unproductive information about banks and the economy.

The role deposit insurance plays in the prevention of bank runs hence depends upon the theoretical setting within which it is analysed. In a setting where withdrawals are viewed as random, triggered by irrational behaviour of depositors, deposit insurance is a mechanism which by transferring wealth across diverse types of agents, eliminates the incentive to participate in a run. It keeps an aggregate shock like a sunspot from destabilizing banking and thus the economy in general.

In a setting where depositors' behaviour is rational and withdrawals are rational responses to the damaged perception of risk, occurring on a large size because of the asymmetry of information regards individual bank performance, deposit insurance acts to alleviate asymmetric information problems. Depositors have smaller incentive to participate in a run.

What is interesting to point out is that the two different theoretical lines[22] agree that the provision of a private mechanism of protection by local clearinghouses in the absence of a central bank and of deposit insurance, was effective in responding to bank panics. The form of private insurance arrangements provided by bank coalitions in the pre-Federal Reserve System, represents an example of spontaneous market regulation against banking instability.

2.2 SYSTEMIC RISK AS A SOURCE OF FINANCIAL INSTABILITY

The theoretical models which have been provided by the literature to explain banking panics find the crucial cause-effect relationship in the behaviour of depositors. The depositors' behaviour is irrational, in the view of non-fundamental theory. Panics are induced by random deposit withdrawals triggered by anything that causes agents to anticipate a run.[23] In the fundamental theory, on the contrary, panics are systematic events resulting from a rational response of depositors to well-defined economic signals. Although these views differ from each other fundamentally, they each identify depositor behaviour as the source of panics.

It may be argued that another potential source of large banking runs and financial system instability exists.

The rationale for this argument arises from looking at banks in their interrelationships rather than in their role as intermediary institutions, providing services to allow borrowers and lenders to meet at lower costs. Our aim here is to shift the focus from the portfolio management to the payment transfer function of banks.

In the first chapter we argued that banks provide a unique role of combining the holding of illiquid assets with the issuing of liquid liability. This function, while enabling banks to provide useful services, is at the same time a weakness. The reasoning, therefore, was based on the bank and its relationship with borrowers and lenders. Depositors' large withdrawals force banks to sell assets at fire-sale prices; consequently, firms are forced to interrupt productive investments. The results of this process are high costs of intermediation and high social and economic costs. Now, the reasoning is based on the bank and its relationship within other banks, with the aim to point out the bank susceptibility to instability because of the weakness inherent to bank-to-bank transactions. In other words, it is possible to argue that the risk of banking system instability can be caused by the inefficiencies of the interbank market as well as by depositors' large withdrawals.

2.2.1 Banks and Payment Systems

Crucial to our analysis is the existence of automatized systems of funds transfer which enable banks to manage an increasing amount of payment transfers without adjusting their reserves at the same rate. In 1970 the United States financial system was involved in an amount of transfers approximately equal to the amount of the banks' aggregate reserve balances at the Federal Reserve. Years later, in 1980, the amount of the transfers were 26 times as large, so that the average dollar on balance turned over 26 times daily.[24] The United States experience is not dissimilar from other countries when the volume of transfers has risen very rapidly whereas reserves did not.

Moreover, some payment systems use electronic transfer systems (Chips in United States, Sterling and ECU in Europe) which operate on the principle of end-of-day net settlement. This means that final settlement obligations are generated by participants at the end of the day as they make and receive payments, and that intra-day net debit and credit positions do not reflect the final settlement. In these systems, therefore, daylight exposures occur and they are created as part of normal operations.

Although technical devices are available that allow on-line real-time transfer, the end-of-day settlement processing is banks' daylight overdraft. Interbank transfers do not flow evenly through the day and banks can make payments in anticipation of funds to be received later the same day. When the central bank is not directly involved in the payments in such a way as to be able to absorb any losses resulting from a bank failure, by becoming a general creditor of the failed bank, the failure of one overdrafting bank will cause one or more of the other banks to fail. A systemic risk exists.

Therefore, if bank failure occurred, the overdrafts which are generated

57

daily by the smooth operations of the payment system could become disruptive for the financial system.

Various systems of payment operate within different countries. Many of them are similar to Fedwire, the wire transfer system operated by the Federal Reserve System, in that payments are made through reserve or clearing accounts at the central bank during the business day. In these systems banks may transfer their reserve balances to other banks that have similar accounts. In the Fedwire system, Federal Reserve banks transfer reserves to receiving banks even if the reserve balance of the sending bank is insufficient to cover the transfers. Transfers over Fedwire become final when the receiving banks are notified of the transfers. Thus, if a sending bank should fail while its reserve account was overdrawn, the Federal Reserve would have no claim on banks that received reserves from the failed bank over Fedwire. In this system daylight overdrafts represent intra-day negative reserve account balances on Fedwire and the failure of a participating bank creates a credit risk for the Reserve bank.

Payments over a system operated by the central bank involve no systemic risk. A settlement failure is absorbed by central bank funds.

In other countries, private interbank transfer systems operate. In the United States, in addition to Fedwire, the Clearing House Interbank Payment System (Chips) transfers funds among about 140 members, which include U.S.-chartered banks and foreign banks. In this system, participants send and receive electronic payment messages during the day through a central computer. Unlike the case of Fedwire, however, no funds are transferred nor are accounts debited or credited at the time Chips payment messages are exchanged. As we have seen, net obligations in private networks, as well as in Chips, are settled at the end of the day. In the case of Chips it occurs through a special account, the New York Clearinghouse and the Fed.

In this end-of-day settlement system, all participants begin daily operations with zero credit and debit positions and intra-day exposures represent uncovered net debit positions. In this system the settlement failure of a participating bank can precipitate the failure of others by making their debit position worse. The staff of the Board of Governors has defined this systemic risk as "... the potential cumulative impact on the liquidity and solvency of a large number of institutions resulting from a failure by one institution to settle its net debit position in a private

58

network, and the resultant implications for the stability of the banking system, for the firms dependent on the functioning of the payments mechanism and for the operation of financial markets generally"[25].

This definition stresses the existing causal relationship between systemic risk and financial system instability we have pointed out above. The vulnerability of bank-to-bank transactions when not effectuated by real-time transfers systems is, in fact, a potential source of bank intermediation instability.

The risk of settlement failure is very low. For settlement failure to occur, a bank must be unable to obtain the funds necessary to settle its position either through the discount window or from other banks. It means that the bank failure would have to occur during a day, and a failure of this sort could probably occur only if significant 'osses due to fraud or theft were uncovered during the day.

Central bank intervention to ensure settlement is viewed as a practicable way to counteract systemic risk. Nevertheless, central bank intervention would not be without consequences. If the central bank postpones the failure by opening the discount window, the settlement risk would be transferred to the central bank and other creditors of the bank. Network participants would receive their payments, but the central bank would be exposed to the extent of its discount window loan. In this case the systemic risk due to payments system failure would be averted, but there would be still the effects of losses suffered by other creditors. On the other hand if the central bank is expected to act to avert a settlement failure, banks would have no incentive to monitor their net credit positions with other banks. Allowing weaker banks to run very large net debit positions may increase the probability of systemic collapse if a settlement failure occurs.

A settlement failure has never occurred. Its consequences are hence unknown. Furthermore in 1986 the Federal Reserve implemented a system of quantitative limits on overdrafts and a programme of upgrading internal credit, monitoring, and operational controls on both interbank overdrafts and overdrafts on customer accounts. Recently, these policies have been re-examined with the aim of improving them and averting any risk for the payment system. Nevertheless, the disruptive effects of a settlement failure in terms of systemic risk are evident and can be further examined by a deeper analysis of a settlement failure and the implications of such a failure on other banks.

2.2.2 The magnitude of systemic risk

Here we will discuss the operation of the payment system and the risk that arises from depository institutions' use of the payment system.

Let us suppose a payment system where the central bank is not involved and hence no device to absorb any losses resulting from failure by a bank exists. In particular let us consider a provisional-wire transfer network such as Chips.

In Chips, as we have seen, members send and receive payment messages during the day; they begin daily operations with zero credit and debit positions and no funds are actually transferred to cover the payment messages until the end of the business day. At the day's end the transfer funds are settled. Banks in net debit positions – that is banks whose value of payment messages sent exceeds the value of payment messages received – transfer funds from their accounts at their Federal Reserve Bank to a reserve account maintained by Chips at the Federal Reserve Bank of New York. Banks in net credit positions, on the contrary, receive reserve transfers from that account.

Pursuant to Chips rules, the inability of a bank to settle its end-of-day net position triggers a special process termed unwinding. All payment messages to and from that bank are cancelled; since payment messages do not reflect intra-day extensions of credit among banks but only temporary payments, they may be unwound at the end of the day. Nevertheless, a settlement failure could expose the remaining participants to losses. In fact, if remaining banks depositors have withdrawn balances during the day based on payment messages from the defaulting bank, the remaining banks might be unable to recover the withdrawn funds.

Removing the transfers sent and received by a participant will have varying impacts on different participants depending on their net position with the institution that fails to settle.

By using simple balance sheet entries it is possible to illustrate how transactions through Chips affect the exposure of member banks to potential losses, that is, how banks, by participating in Chips assume a risk which does not depend upon their behaviour. Let us suppose a system with three banks A, B and C.[26] Banks A and B begin the day with deposits of $100 and reserve of $10, and their balance sheet entries are illustrated in Table 2.2.

Table 2.2: Risk created by the transfer of funds over Chips

1. Balance sheets at the start of day:

Bank A			Bank B		
Reserves $10	Deposits $100		Reserves $10	Deposits $100	
Other assets	100	Net worth	10	Other assets	100	Net worth	10

Bank A		Bank B	
Reserves $10	Deposits $100	Reserves $10	Deposits $100
Other assets 100	Net worth 10	Other assets 100	Net worth 10

2. Depositor at Bank A transfers $25 of Bank B, transaction over Chips:

Bank A		Bank B	
Reserves $10	Deposits $75	Reserves $10	Deposits $125
Other assets 100	Reserves payable 25	Reserves receivable 25	Net worth 10
	Net worth 10	Other assets 100	

3.Depositor at Bank B transfers $25 to depositor of Bank C, over Chips:

Bank A		Bank B	
Reserves $10	Deposits $100	Reserves $10	Deposits $125
Reserves receivable 25	Receives payable 25	Reserves receivable 25	Net worth 10
Other assets 100	Net worth 10	Other assets 100	

Source: Gilbert (1989)

The first transaction by bank A in the current day is a deposit transfer. A depositor of bank A sends $25 to a depositor of bank B. Bank A debits the deposit account of that customer for $25. Since the transfer occurs over Chips, and banks do not report their balance sheets on the intra-day basis, there is no official term for the offsetting liability entry in this transaction. Thus banks A and B balance sheets are modified as follows: for bank A the deposits item has decreased to $75 and a special item – reserve payable – of $25 indicates the deposit transfer; for bank B a new asset item – reserve reccivable – indicates the message of transfer and the deposits item has risen to $125. No real transfer has occurred. In the next transaction, a depositor of bank B directs it to send $25 to a depositor of bank C over Chips. If no more transactions occur during the day among the banks, the end-of-day settlement will have a zero impact on the reserve account of bank B. Bank A is in a net debit position and its reserve account will be debited for $25. Bank C, on the other hand, is in a net credit position and it will have its reserve account credited by $25. Assuming a 10 per cent reserve ratio, bank A has to increase its reserve balance to meet the settlement at the end of the day.

Suppose that bank A is unable to increase its reserve balance. This situation could create a liquidity problem for bank B. If bank A fails to settle, Chips' rules call for unwinding all transaction involving bank A and settling the transaction among the remaining banks. This settlement involves a transfer of $25 in reserves from bank B to bank C. Bank B has only $10 in its reserve account, and unless bank B borrows $25 from the market or from central bank, such a settlement cannot take place. In this case all Chips transaction for the day will be cancelled. This example indicates that the unwinding of transactions with one Chips bank which cannot meet its payment obligation would make a high percentage of other member banks unable to meet their commitments on Chips. Bank C, which has no direct transactions with the defaulting bank A, assumes the risk of loss, because the default bank A makes bank B illiquid.

It could be shown, however, that a Federal Reserve intervention by lending alternatively either to bank A or to bank B does not prevent the system from suffering losses (Gilbert, 1989).

The example we have illustrated provides a simulation of systemic risk involved in the operation of a payment system.

Going further, Humphrey (1986) quantified the systemic risk inherent in an end-of-day settlement system, showing its potential magnitude. The concern is that if there were a failure to settle one or more of the large daylight overdraft, that occur in a payment system such as Chips, the smooth operation of the system and the financial system as a whole would be significantly disrupted. Evidence to support this contention is provided by results from a settlement-failure simulation exercise performed by Federal Reserve staff. The simulation considers the effects of a failure of a Chips participant on the net positions of the other participants. Using historical data, transaction activity for a given day is recorded, and as a consequence of a bank settlement failure, all transfers to and from that bank are removed, according to Chips rules. Since there is no way to simulate fully a situation in which other institutions perceive a problem and partially adjust their exposure, the failure of a participant in a net credit position is assumed. The net credit position of a bank participating in the network results, in fact, from a relatively small extension of gross daylight credit to that bank from the other participants. It means that the network members have perceived the risk and the failure is relatively unexpected.

The simulation is performed on a randomly selected business day during January 1983 by using the actual record of all transactions. The selected failure participant has a net credit position of $321 million in the day in which the failure is assumed to occur. The settlement position of all institutions before and after the removal of all payment to and from the failed bank are calculated.

The simulation is performed over a number of interactions, and in order to pursue the settlement revision process to its ultimate conclusion over these interactions, a standard assumption is used. If a participant experiences a position deterioration equal to or exceeding its capital and it is in a net debit position in the revised settlement, then it is presumed to be unable to settle. Thus, for cash interactions a revised net settlement position for all participants is computed after removing any participant that failed (according to the assumption), along with all transfers to and from it.

For the first revised settlement, which occurs after the simulation of the selected bank failure, twenty-four institutions have settlement obligations that have increased by more than the amount of their capital and have ended up in a net debit position. Table 2.3 shows the original settlement position of each of these institutions (column a), and the magnitude of the settlement position change, calculated as the ratio of the settlement position change to the institution's capital (column b).

Table 2.4 shows that the results of the subsequent interactions are required before any participant fails to meet the criterion stated by the assumption. The unexpected failure of a bank participating in Chips induces, according to this simulation, the failure of fifty other participants.

Table 2.3: Simulation 1: Institutions affected by a Chips participant failure during the first interaction

	Original Net Settlement Position (millions of $) (a)	Ratio of position change to capital (b)
1	86.6	22.7
2	18.5	21.4
3	−16.8	1.5
4	23.1	2.2
5	−27.7	4.5
6	−28.7	8.2
7	−15.2	2.2
8	−71.8	1.7
9	−15.8	19.1
10	−160.7	1.8
11	3.5	4.2
12	−4.4	8.4
13	−21.5	15.8
14	40.8	31.4
15	−25.8	7.5
16	0	12.4
17	−3.1	7.1
18	−2.7	3.0
19	2.0	11.1
20	−37.8	1.4
21	−378.5	2.9
22	6.6	7.7
23	−39.0	12.1
24	177.3	15.4

Source: Humphrey (1986)

Table 2.4: Simulation 1: Total number of failed Chips participants

Interaction	Number of failed* institutions
1	24
2	12
3	10
4	3
5	1
6	0
Total	50

Source: Humphrey (1986)

* An institution is considered failed when it faces a net debit position in the revised settlement and its net settlement obligation exceeds its capital.

Because of the assumption, the results of Table 2.5 overstate the magnitude of the problem which could develop, to the extent that institutions can on average sustain settlement position changes in excess of their capital. On the contrary, the results understate the magnitude of the problem to the extent that the institution, for example, withdraws from the settlement when its revised settlement obligation increases by more than 10 per cent of its capital. This simulation shows the quantitative effects of systemic risk existing in the Chips network.

Going further, the Humphrey simulation also gives some qualitative indications. A second simulation is repeated on a different day. The aim of this exercise is to assess the sensitivity of the simulation results to the transaction activity on the particular day used in the first simulation. Tables 2.5 and 2.6 show the results of this second simulation.

Table 2.5: Simulation 2: Institutions affected by a Chips participant failure during the first interaction

	Original Net Settlement Position (millions of $) (a)	Ratio of position change to capital (b)
1	9.4	4.7
2	−60.3	13.4
3	16.6	5.8
4	5.3	1.2
5	−23.0	3.0
6	13.9	3.5
7	−16.6	1.8
8	58.8	4.3
9	−11.0	1.3
10	0.2	1.5
11	−75.4	4.7
12	−16.6	1.9
13	2.0	8.8
14	−56.0	3.6
15	−91.0	1.2
16	−2.6	103.4

Source: Humphrey (1986)

Source: Humphrey (1986)

Table 2.6: Simulation 2: Total number of
failed Chips participants

Interaction	Number of failed* institutions
1	16
2	11
3	12
4	9
5	1
6	0
Total	49

* An institution is considered failed when it faces a net debit position in the revised settlement and its net settlement obligation exceeds its capital.

Although the results confirm the domino effects of an unexpected failure of a large Chips participant on the network system, nevertheless, some fundamental differences arise. Fewer institutions experience an increase in their settlement position obligations in excess of their capital and are in a net debit position for the revised settlement in the first interaction. In addition, the average ratio of position change to capital is somewhat lower for the second simulation.

These differences can be explained in part because of the different net credit positions of the failed settling participant in the second simulation. It is roughly three times the same participant's net credit position for the first simulation ($921 million). Furthermore the total dollar value of messages sent on the day of the second simulation is significantly lower than on the day of the first simulation.

Nevertheless, in comparing the consequence of a failure of the same participant on two different days a fundamental difference emerges. The affected institutions are different.

As Humphrey points out, in view of the correspondent relationships among institutions, one might expect that those affected by a particular institution's failure would be fairly constant; in fact, there is a fair amount of variation.

Only five failed institutions of the first interactions are common to the first and second simulation (Tables 2.3 and 2.5) Similarly, sixteen institutions which are included in the total of fifty failed in the first simulation are not included in the forty-nine of the second (Tables 2.4 and 2.6).

These results suggest that the institutions most likely to be affected by a particular institution's failure cannot be readily identified beforehand.

In conclusion, the risk associated with daylight overdrafts in a large payment system is difficult to quantify because of the interdependence of institutions operating in the same system. In addition this interdependence is dynamic. It means that the systemic risk exposure of institutions varies from day to day. Systemic risk is not measurable and it is not identifiable. These conclusions have important consequences in terms of financial system stability and in terms of political implications. In 1988, on an average day, about 1,100 US depositor institutions generated some $104 billion in funds transfer daylight overdrafts on the payment system.[27] A settlement failure has never occurred, but its effects on the financial market could be significant.

In this respect the experience of clearinghouses in the pre-Fed era represents an example of the importance of the interbank market stability in the banking system.

In a less sophisticated and developed system, such as the National Banking System, the private bank associations have played a unique role by ensuring the normal flow of interbank operations. By providing stable relationships among members the system as a whole was able to face instability arising from depositor runs.

The evolution of the financial system, with the associated growth of new and different types of financial transactions, may represent an increasing threat, to the extent that some other sources of instability join with traditional sources.

The evolution of the system of payments, based on the temporary transfers of funds, represents an example of this. Depositors' behaviour is no longer the unique source of banking panics.

2.3 THE SUCCESSFUL EXPERIENCE OF CLEARINGHOUSE ASSOCIATIONS

Bank liability insurance organised at a local level by clearinghouses has been operating in the United States for nearly a century, starting in 1853 in New York. During this period many banks were able to survive when runs occurred.

Many bank panics took place during the National Banking Era, as historical evidence shows, but their effects on financial intermediation and their macroeconomic impact did not approach the severity of the subsequent era panics, namely those in the depression. Table 2.7 shows the effects of six of the major bank panics which occurred in the pre-1914 era. It compares the number of National Banks, divided by regions, existing prior to panics with the number of their failures during panics. The evidence is that panics in the National Banking Era did not induce widespread bank failures.

The reason for that may be the existing mechanism provided by the market in the form of private banking associations. As Gorton and Mullineaux (1987) pointed out the evolution of commercial bank clearinghouses from simple places where representatives of all banks in the same city met to settle accounts with all associated banks, to insurance arrangements, reflects an endogenous regulatory response to the problem associated with the asymmetric distribution of information in the banking industry. During banking panics the clearinghouses united banks into an organisation resembling a single firm which produced deposit insurance.

The initial function of clearinghouses was to economise on costs of check clearing. Prior to the formation of the clearinghouses, banks collected checks and other instruments by daily exchange and settlement with other banks. The establishment of clearinghouses created an organised market where at the local level, exchange between banks could occur through one other party – the clearinghouse itself. But together with providing a check clearing service, these organisations were also capable of producing a by-product, that is information.

In fact, they had an exploitable information advantage over their customers concerning the quality of bank liabilities. The raising of demand deposits relative to bank notes, furthermore, contributed to enlarging the role of the clearinghouses. Bank notes, because of their contractual characteristic,[28] had stimulated the creation of a secondary market where they were exchanged at a discount against specie – the bank note market, through the prices and exchange rates of different bank notes, revealed information about the specific issuing banks. On the contrary, unlike bank notes, demand deposits did not allow the development of a private secondary market with allocation power. The pricing of a check claim, because of the double claim involved in it, on a bank and on an agent's account at that bank, involved, in fact, the high costs of gathering information about the check writer and his bank. In

Table 2.7: Number of national banks and national bank failures during panics, by region, 1873–1907

Region	1873 Bank	Failures	1884 Bank	Failures	1890 Bank	Failures	1893 Bank	Failures	1896 Bank	Failures	1907 Bank	Failures
New England	506	0	565	1	583	0	595	2	586	0	482	0
East	590	3	715	2	851	0	933	2	951	3	1,424	1
South	164	3	248	1	521	1	586	15	561	6	1,283	1
Middle West	664	2	775	3	981	0	1,090	9	1,067	12	1,841	4
West	51	1	148	1	458	8	460	1	378	10	1,089	0
Pacific	10	0	40	0	146	1	177	7	133	3	293	0
Total	1,985	9	2,491	8	3,540	10	3,841	49	3,676	34	6,412	6
Reserve centre Banks		2		1		0		3		4		0

Source: Calomiris and Gorton (1990)

this case clearinghouses, because of their special position relative to their member banks, could provide a non price allocation system.[29]

Clearinghouses eventually replaced a market-based mechanism of control with an hierarchical mechanism, realised on the basis of control and monitoring of members. In these evolved organisations, member banks were strictly supervised. They were subjected to an admission test and to periodic exams and they could be expelled from the clearinghouse when their probability of nonperformance was high. Furthermore, the clearinghouses were able to audit members' books. The new configuration of clearinghouses, imposed by the practical exigencies of informational externalities, created the framework for the insurance role they would perform during panics.

At the onset of a systemic panic, the clearinghouse suppressed bank-specific information by suspending the publication of individual balance sheets. The balance sheet of the entire clearinghouse association was published in order to signal the clearinghouse's united effort to preserve the banking system. This represented the first step towards the metamorphosis of clearinghouses into a single firm-like organisation, uniting member banks in a hierarchical structure (Gorton, 1988).

The absence of a central bank and the presence of a fractional reserve system caused a bank run to be a threat for the entire banking system. A widespread desire to convert demand deposits into currency depleted the reserves of banks, forcing them to liquidate their loans. In this environment clearinghouses operated by recycling funds from deposit gaining to deposit losing banks, preventing a run on one bank from setting off runs on other banks.

The technical mechanism whereby clearinghouses intervened, creating in practice temporary currency, was the creation of clearinghouse loan certificates. They were a kind of special securities that allowed banks' assets to be transferred in such a way as to signal to depositors their value.

Clearinghouse loan certificates were temporary loans made to banks, upon receipt of sufficient collateral, and carried an interest charge. They could be used to settle clearinghouse balances, by acting in practice as reserves. This substitution for currency in clearinghouse settlements allowed banks to use currency to satisfy depositors' demands for cash or to meet other obligations.

When a panic occurred and banks faced widespread demand for

currency they applied to the Clearinghouse Loans Committee, submitting part of their portfolios as collateral. If the collateral was considered sufficient then certificates were issued amounting to a percentage, usually 75%, of the market value of the collateral. In practice bank assets were transformed in to more liquid securities without being liquidated and at a price equal to the discount rate, given by the difference between their real market value and the value of the loans certificates issued on them.

The joint circumstance that loan certificates were both backed by discounted assets and represented claims on the issuing clearinghouse, that is, they were a joint liability of the member banks, made them acceptable in the clearing process. If a member bank failed and the collateral was worth less than the member's outstanding loan certificates, the loss was shared among the remaining members in proportion to each member's capital. At the end of the panic the failed members were expelled from the clearinghouse, but until that time they were part of the organisation. Immediate expulsion would have had high externality effects by disrupting the unity of information on member bank performances. Thus, during bank panics, the clearinghouses operated by administering the internal allocation of resources in order to prevent depositors from irrational withdrawals.

The scheme provided by the emergency operations of the clearinghouses, which experienced eight panics from 1857 to 1914, presented the features of an insurance scheme, performing many of the functions of insurance funds.

It prevented financial collapse, and provided continuity of transactions throughout the banking system during the crisis, by insulating the payment system from individual and economy wide bank runs.

Furthermore, it provided a risk-sharing arrangement, whereby member banks insured each other to the extent of their capital. Although the interest rate on loan certificates and the discount on collateral did not vary over banks or assets, the system was able to ensure that banks would not take advantage of the coinsurance arrangement. In fact, as the arrangement was intended to allocate resources to all members under the same conditions, even those which were considered nearly failed, it could have induced some banks to take excessive risk. However some devices were provided to prevent this occurrence.

One of these devices was inherent in the clearinghouse partnership. Self-imposed regulations imposed reserve ratios and restrictions on

71

portfolio holdings. Furthermore the banks had a strong incentive to monitor the actions of their partners and to eject members who broke the rules. Secondly, during panics, by issuing loan certificates, the clearinghouses could, at their discretion, demand additional security and requisition aid for particularly troubled banks, in order to balance the advantage arising from the mutual insurance with the individual contribution to the group loss probability.

Another device available to clearinghouses to stem panics was the restriction of bank deposit convertibility into currency. This action limited the ability of depositors to withdraw their deposits from the banking system, but the intermediation process continued, ensuring that the banking system remained operational. This device was essentially intended to allow the price of currency to increase relative to deposits, thus reducing the currency demand during panic periods. Furthermore, the restriction or the suspension of convertibility signalled the clearinghouse's belief that further liquidation of bank assets to acquire currency were not in the interests of either the banks or their depositors.

On two occasions, in particular during the panics of 1893 and 1907, clearinghouse intervention was very similar to the modern insurance scheme. The clearinghouses monetised bank portfolios by issuing loan certificates directly to the public. This strategy was induced by the limited amount of currency released through use of "normal" loan certificates. If there were not large enough normal loan certificates, the currency released could not signal to depositors that one-to-one deposit exchange rate was accurate, and the organizational structure of clearinghouses could not be successful.

Issuing loan certificates directly to the public did not involve replacing gold in the clearing process. Instead, by monetising bank portfolios, a large amount of money could be created and issued to the public in exchange for demand deposits. The "new" certificates were certified checks made payable through the clearinghouses. Depositors were willing to accept these certificates rather than currency because the loan certificates insured them against individual bank failure. The problem of the asymmetric information about bank specific risk was solved, leaving only the risk that the issuing clearinghouses would fail. Since the circulating loan certificates made bank-specific risk irrelevant to deposits and they were not agent specific, unlike deposits, a secondary market for these claims developed, allowing the risk of single clearinghouse failure priced.

In this way a medium of exchange backed by illiquid means – single bank assets – and the substituting of currency was provided through the intervention of the clearinghouses. During the panic of 1893 about 100 million dollars of clearinghouse hand-to-hand money was issued, reaching 2.5% of the money stock. The panic of 1907 had approximately 500 million dollars in monitored bank assets traded as currency, nearly 4.5% of the measured money stock.

In conclusion, the experience of State clearinghouses was successful. The private bank coalitions were effective in monitoring banks, in intervening with ad hoc instruments to provide liquidity to the banking system in an emergency, and then in mitigating panics. Their success was founded on their ability to self-regulate and their authority over the members. Strictly speaking, they provided, in an unregulated market, a private discipline. Both imposed rules of behaviour and the clearinghouses' ability to intervene in the market with a high degree of discretional power during panics made the system of the private bank associations an effective mechanism for coordinating bank responses to panics, built on the members' consent.

But the clearinghouses legitimacy, created by general consent, did not prevent some questions concerning their legality from arising – the distribution of loan certificates, though providing temporary currency very useful to meet depositors' claims, and undertaken with the tacit approval of the authorities, was technically illegal. Furthermore, as Timberlake (1984) pointed out, the clearinghouses' currency seemed to arise out of nothing. It was difficult to understand how a clearinghouse system could create emergency currency without seeming to have an emergency reserve on which to base it.

At the same time, since the private money producing the industry's answer to panics was not able to eliminate completely the financial instability arising from runs, and it was highly visible in terms of social and private costs, ways were sought to improve the existing structure. The establishment of the Federal Reserve System, serving as a national clearinghouse, was the institutional answer to the private associations. The Fed was thought of as operating the same way as State clearinghouses, but, by having direct access to the reserves of all banks of the United States, it was intended to expedite the recycling of runs across all the banks in the country. The liquidity role of the clearinghouses during the crisis was thereby transferred to the Fed, restricting local clearinghouse functions to payment operations among banks. Contrary to expectations, the Fed was not able to play the insurance role of the State clearinghouses, and its assumed effectiveness in maintaining confidence in the banking system was unequivocally disproven by the events of the '30s. Thus, it became necessary to support it with the establishment of the Federal Deposit Insurance Corporation, splitting the responsibility for financial system stability.

NOTES

1. Diamond and Dybvig provide a modern version of the theory that in its traditional form dates back to Noyes (1909), Gibbos (1968), Kindleberger (1978) et al.
2. Diamond and Dybvig refer always to a pure strategy Nash equilibrium.
3. The definition "non-fundamental" has been employed by Tallman (1988), in defining "non-economic".
4. Calomiris and Gorton (1990).
5. Calomiris (1989), Chari and Jannathan (1988), Gorton (1987, 1989), Gorton and Mullineaux (1987), Jacklin and Bhattacharya (1988).
6. Such as Gorton (1988), Tallman (1988), Calomiris and Gorton (1990).
7. Calomiris and Gorton (1990).
8. Bryant's model is a complicated version of Samuelson's (1958) pure consumption-loans model.
9. In presenting the model of Diamond and Dybvig we consider also the version provided by Chari (1989), to the extent that it is useful to clarify and to evidence some aspects of the original model.
10. The technology has constant returns to scale.
11. Chari (1989).
12. See Jacklin (1986).
13. The net payment to those who withdraw at $T = 1$ determines also the asset liquidation policy. Furthermore, any tax collected in excess of that needed to meet withdrawals at $T = 1$ is ploughed back into the bank.
14. Where $t = p_1 t_1 + p_2 t_2$.
15. X_1 and X_2 are equivalent to the V_1 and V_2 defined in Diamond and Dybving model.
16. $X_1 < X_2$, so that $X_2/X_2 > 1$.
17. Calomiris and Gorton (1990).
18. The definitions assume a binding cash-in-advance constraint on the consumer, with deposits as the only way of saving.

19. By assuming $\pi_t \geq 0$, the asymmetry of deposit contracts is introduced in the model. Depositors do not have ex-ante information about the positive $(\pi_t = 0)$ or negative $(\pi_t > 0)$ performances.
20. The model (d), (e) and (f) is not jointly estimable because of the truncation of (e) and the effect of that truncation on (f). Thus, the first step in estimating the model is the estimation of the capital loss on deposit, equation (e), the fitted value of which enters equation (6).
21. Data for consumption and capital losses on deposits, for example, are not available. Pig iron consumption and loss on assets compounded or sold pursuant to court order are respectively used as proxies.
22. See Chari (1989) and Gorton (1988).
23. Diamond and Dybvig (1983) p.410.
24. Benston et al (1986).
25. Dudley (1986).
26. The example follows the Gilbert (1989) simulation.
27. Humphrey (1989)
28. Bank notes involved a contract between the bearer and the bank to redeem the face value of the note in specie at the bank. For this, bank notes could be exchanged by brokers at discounted rates and then redeemed by them at par at the issuing bank.
29. On this point see Gorton (1985).

3 The fundamental dilemma of deposit insurance

The previous chapters described possible beneficial effects of deposit insurance, under different explanations for its provision. Nevertheless, whatever explanation, as with any government intervention designed to enhance the market mechanism, there are potentially adverse effects from the implementation of deposit insurance.

This problem is related to the effective impact of deposit insurance on banks' behaviour, in particular, and on depositors' expectations in general. By providing a guarantee that depositors are not subject to losses, deposit insurance removes the incentive to participate in a bank run. However, as recent studies have clearly established, the present structure of most deposit insurance schemes changes the incentive structure of insured depositors in ways that will tend to increase the risk exposure of individual depository institutions, increase the likelihood of losses by the insurance agency and decrease equitable treatment of institutions in the payment of insurance premia.

Deposit insurance and present available technology virtually eliminate the incentive for insured depositors to monitor the banks' risk-taking. Deposit insurance also reduces incentives for monitoring by demand depositors in the largest banks. As a result there is an increased incentive for banks to take risks in the hope of profiting thereby.

Therefore, deposit insurance affects the allocation of resources in an economy by transferring wealth between banks debt holders and shareholders. In general, shareholders/debt holders conflict issues arise because banks' debtholders may not be able to perfectly infer the true risk levels chosen by shareholders. In particular, the conflict issue is further complicated by institutional design and arrangements of deposit insurance which give banks additional incentive to surreptitiously increase the risk structure of their portfolios. When a deposit insurance is binding, banks do not have to be concerned about safety of depositors' funds and they impose extra risk on society.

The case for banking regulation arises as a necessary complement to deposit insurance. However, regulation itself is not costless in terms of banks' efficiency and resources allocation.

3.1 THE MORAL HAZARD PROBLEM

The fundamental dilemma of any deposit insurance system is that it cannot protect depositors against banks failures caused by illiquidity without protecting depositors against banks' failures caused by poor performance of a bank's loans and investments. Because depositors are guaranteed against the second type of failure as well as the first, current deposit insurance systems distort the behaviour of banks.

Furthermore existing institutional design and arrangements of deposit insurance systems are of central importance to the distortions of both depositors and banks behaviour towards risk. First, insurance of any type makes the insured somewhat less careful because the costs or penalties from losses are perceived to be less than in the absence of deposit insurance. In addition to that, depositors insurance makes depositors less careful about evaluating and monitoring the financial integrity of their banks and thereby reduces the degree of market discipline that banks exert.

Secondly, premiums for deposit insurance are a constant proportion of the total domestic deposits of the insured banks rather than proportional to the risk exposure of the institutions. This means that, because losses on risky opportunities are, on average, larger than losses on less risky opportunities, a flat rate premium structure results in an inequitable treatment of insured banks. Risky institutions pay the same insurance coverage than less risky institutions. Furthermore, because the expected revenue payoff on risky opportunities is greater than on less risky opportunities, while the cost of insured funds to finance these investments do not increase proportionately, the expected net income payoff will also be greater to banks taking on more risky investments. Thus, under the current system of fixed-rate deposit insurance banks have a large incentive to take actions that increase its probability of failure.

Thirdly, because depositors need not be concerned about the safety of their funds up to the maximum amount insured, the provision of deposit insurance allows banks that are economically insolvent but not yet legally declared insolvent and closed, to attract additional funds. It means that market discipline fails in timely driving unsound banks out of the market.

Finally, insurance agency's policy of handling bankruptcy has in practice protected contractually uninsured depositors, by arranging very often purchase and mergers rather than making direct payments to depositor. The extension of de jure insurance to a de facto coverage of 100 per cent of deposits, by increasing insured depositors, prevents the uninsured depositors' monitoring, from working in preventing banks moral hazard.

Thus, the institutional and structural aspects of deposit insurance – fixed premium and high account coverage – together with the actual policies of intervention in bank failures, increase the moral hazard problem by increasing the banks risk incentive and increase the insurance agency risk of losses. Deposit insurance, therefore, involves a basic trade-off between the possibility of destructive bank runs and negative externalities. In particular lack of depositor discipline provides banks the opportunity to arrange its portfolio so as to increase its expected profits at the expense of the insurer. The incentive for excessive risk-taking can be analysed at first, with a very simple example.[1]

Let us consider a bank funded with $90 of deposits. Suppose that the bank has a choice between two portfolio assets which have the same expected value. The "safe" portfolio will return $100 with certainty and the "risky" portfolio will pay $80 if a bad state occurs and will pay $120 if a good state occurs. If the bank chooses the safe portfolio, its value is $10, that is the difference between the return of the investment and the value of deposits ($100-$90). If the bank chooses the risky portfolio, its value to the shareholder is either zero or $30 with the same probability ($\frac{1}{2}$). In the first case the return on the investment, $80, is not enough to repay depositors, $90. In the second, the difference between the return on the investment is $120 and it is greater than deposits. Therefore, the expected value of the bank is:

$$(\tfrac{1}{2}) \ \$0 + (\tfrac{1}{2})(\$120 - \$90) = \$15$$

If a fixed premium deposit insurance covers the risk of any losses, banks will maximise the expected return to shareholders by selecting the risky portfolio.

In the example above, the risk to incur losses is only on the insurer. Let us consider the cost of providing the insurance. If the bank chooses the safe portfolio, there is no cost because the bank cannot fail. If the bank chooses the risky portfolio, the cost of insurance is given by the payment to depositors net of the value of assets ($90 – $80 = $10) if the bad state occurs and equal to zero if the good state occurs. In this case the bank will be able to pay depositors. The risky portfolio gives to the insurer an expected cost equal to:

$$(\tfrac{1}{2}) \ \$0 + (\tfrac{1}{2}) \ \$10 = \$5$$

By allowing the bank to freely choose their portfolio, the insurer increases the bank expected value from $10 to $15, at its own expenses.

This simple example gives the sight of the problems in terms of excessive risk-taking incentives for banks and in terms of cost for insurance agencies.

The following analysis provides a theoretical framework for the actual impact of deposit insurance on bank behaviour towards risk and its social costs.

3.1.1 Moral hazard towards risky assets

A bank makes two important choices that affect its probability of failure: the riskiness of assets composition, and the ratio of capital to deposits. If the total rate of return on the bank assets is highly variable (risky portfolio) the bank has a high probability of earning high profits but also high probability of incurring large losses. Also, if the bank does not have much capital, relatively small losses may be sufficient to wipe out its capital and force the bank to close. Thus ceteris paribus the probability of failure is greater the riskier the bank assets and the lower the ratio of capital to deposits.[2]

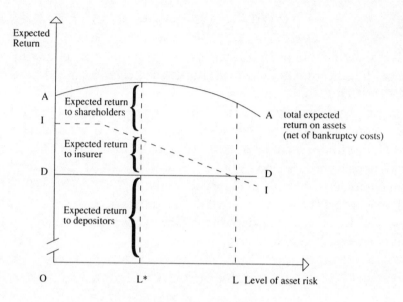

Figure 3.1: Deposit insurance and asset risk

The risk-effect of both these choices – portfolio riskiness and capital adequacy – can be illustrated in Figure 3.1. Let us consider the composition of assets. Insured and uninsured deposits, capital and set of investment opportunities in this model are assumed as given. The horizontal axis of the diagram measures the level of asset risk and each point on the axis corresponds to a different mix of assets with different variability of total return. The level of asset risk chosen by the bank depends on the interest of its shareholders. Only by assuming that shareholders are risk-neutral and that they care about the expected return on their investment but not about the variability of the return, the bank will seek to maximize the total expected return to its shareholders. The behaviour of bank is aimed to

$$\text{Max } E(R) \tag{1}$$

where R = total return on shareholder investment.

80

The bank activity involves insured depositors, uninsured depositors and insurance agency. The total expected return to shareholders, R, is hence equal to:

$$E(R) = E(A) - E(D) - E(U) - E(\text{i}) \qquad (2)$$

that is, $E(R)$ equals the total expected return on the bank assets $E(A)$, minus, the total expected return to all other agents (D = insured depositors; U = uninsured depositors; I = insurance agency).

For each point of the horizontal axis, the curve AA in the figure represents the maximum total expected return the bank could earn on its assets. Each point of AA maximizes the total return for each assets composition.[3]

The curve AA initially slopes upwards. Increasing the level of risk, by choosing a riskier portfolio, it is possible for the bank to increase total expected return on its assets. This makes it more likely that the bank fails. Since the bank is able to charge a relatively high interest on riskier assets, its expected investment revenues will increase. Further increases in risk eventually lower the total expected return on assets, causing the curve AA to turn downward. It means that at a certain point the bank cannot fully compensate for the higher probability of default by charging a higher interest on its assets. The point of maximum for the curve AA is L^* in Figure 3.1.

The total expected return to depositors is represented by the curve OD. By assuming that uninsured depositors can observe exactly how much risk the bank is taking and that they are risk-adverse, the demanded increase in the deposit rate will be just large enough to prevent the expected return on uninsured deposits from falling. The return on insured depositors is guaranteed by the insurance. Thus, the total expected return to depositors is independent of the level of asset risk. The curve DD is horizontal. Furthermore in Figure 3.1 the combined expected return to depositors and the insurance agency is represented by the curve II. The expected return to the insurance agency equals the total insurance premium minus the expected cost to the agency for compensating insured depositors. Since under the current deposit insurance system, the total insurance premium depends only on the level of deposits and not on the portfolio riskiness, the curve is horizontal for low levels of asset risk, where the probability of failure is low. As the level of risk is increased and the probability of failure eventually becomes positive, the expected cost of compensating insured depositors rises above zero and the expected return to the agency begins to fall.

Given this framework, the bank will try to maximise the gap between the curves AA and II, that is the difference between the expected return on its assets and the combined expected return to depositors and insurance agency. The gap is largest and equation (2) is maximised in L, where the curves AA and II have equal slopes.

In Figure 3.1 point L is to the right of L^*. It means that in the presence of deposit insurance the bank will choose a riskier optimum portfolio than it would otherwise.

In L^* the curve AA reaches a maximum and it has zero slope, but, since the curve II has negative slope, the gap between AA and II can always be increased by moving to the right of L^*. Increasing risk beyond L^* reduces the expected return to the insurance agency more than the total expected return on assets, and thus increases the total expected return to shareholders.

The difference between the total expected return on the bank assets at L^* and the total expected return at L represents the increased bank risk-taking induced by deposit insurance. As Keeton (1984) pointed out the moral hazard problem does not necessarily exist for all banks and not for all in the same way. Banks may have different attitudes toward variability in the return on their investments. These different conditions, in terms of Figure 3.1 shift L^* to the right or to the left. However, if the bank faces relatively risky investment opportunities and if shareholders are not highly adverse to variability in their return, the optimal degree of risk will be high enough to cause banks failing. In such case, a moral hazard problem exists, because even a very small increase in risk beyond L^* will tend to benefit shareholders at the expense of the insurer.

The described model shows the effects of deposit insurance by stressing the relevance of the gap between the expected return on assets and the combined expected return to depositors and the insurer. By applying Tobin's model of liquidity preference, Short and O'Driscoll (1984) showed the impact of deposit insurance on bank assets portfolio decisions in a different way. A risk-reward trade-off framework is used in which a financial firm's behaviour depends on the differential return carried on risky over riskless assets.

The differential return earned on the bank's portfolio from investing in risky assets is specified as:

$$R = P_2(r+g) \qquad 0 = P_2 = 1 \qquad (1)$$

where: P_2 = proportion of risky assets in the bank's portfolio;
r = current yield differential between risky and riskless assets;
g = capital gain or loss

By assumption g is a random variable with an expected value of zero – thus, the expected differential return on the portfolio is

$$E(R) = \mu_R = P_2 r \qquad (2)$$

By using the standard deviation as the risk measure, the risk of R depends on the standard deviation of g and on the proportion of funds invested in risky assets:

$$\sigma_R = P_2 \sigma_g \qquad 0 \leq P_2 \leq 1 \qquad (3)$$

At this point the terms on which a bank can obtain a higher yield differential at the cost of incurring additional risk can be derived.[4]

$$\mu_R = \frac{r}{\sigma_g} \sigma_R \qquad \text{for } 0 \leq \sigma_R \leq \sigma_g \qquad (4)$$

Equation (4) describes the opportunity locus, or trade-off between risk and reward for a bank. It can be illustrated graphically as the line OC_1 in Figure 3.2, which shows the rate at which the bank can obtain a higher expected yield for a given risk incurred. Since the bank is assumed to choose two types of assets riskless and risky, the positive slope of OC_1 means that as the bank acquires higher proportion of risky assets, its portfolio becomes riskier and it is compensated by higher expected earnings.

Curve I_1 represents an indifference curve for the bank which maps combinations of expected return and risk that leave the bank at the same level of utility. I_1 has a positive slope because the bank is assumed to be

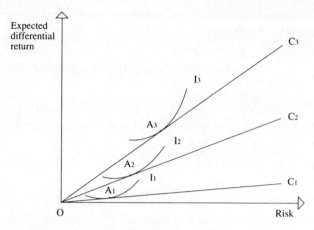

Figure 3.2: Risk-reward trade-off

risk-adverse. That is the bank will accept higher levels of risk only if it receives higher returns. Furthermore, I_1 is concave because amounts of additional returns increase as bank assumes additional risk.

Tangency point, A_1, between opportunity locus and the utility curve, represents the amount of risk and expected differential return that a bank chooses, given the available opportunities and costs constraints it faces. In Figures 3.2, other indifference curves, I_2 and I_3, map other levels of utility.

If the degree of riskiness of the risky assets changes, the slope of the opportunity locus changes as well. In particular a decrease in the riskiness of risky assets causes the OC_1 locus to become steeper. The expected rate differential between risky and riskless assets will be higher for additional risk incurred after the change than before it. The bank, given its risk-reward preferences will increase the proportion of risky assets held in its portfolio. The new equilibrium position will be in A_2. It occurs on the northeast of A_1 assuming that substitution effects dominate income effects in economic decision making.

This risk-reward trade-off analysis is used by Short and O'Driscoll to illustrate the effect of the deposit insurance on portfolio choice made by banks.

The introduction of deposit insurance relieves depositors' fears about the riskiness of the banks' assets portfolio. The expected differential return from incurring more risk is increased for bank. Thus the

84

opportunity locus OC_1 moves to OC_2, becoming the new relevant constraint to the bank, even tough OC_1 is the actual market trade-off between risk a return. Deposit insurance, hence, makes the bank risk-return constraint move further by altering the opportunity locus, and inducing the bank to take more risk.

The price signals about the additional return that would have been required to compensate depositors for the higher risk incurred, do not depend on the market. Furthermore, if the deposit insurance premium is flat and hence unrelated to risk, insurance premiums do not signal the incremental cost of incurring additional risk.

Deposit insurance alters the perception of the actual risk of assets and, a flat premium deposit insurance prevents banks from extimating the cost of incurring additional risk.

These two models, Keeton's and Short and O'Driscoll's provide two different interpretations of the relationships between deposit insurance and bank behaviour toward moral hazard. The former focuses the shifting of cost of failure from shareholders and depositors to the insurer. The latter focuses the alteration effects on risk perception. Both models focus on the portfolio composition.

3.1.2 Moral hazard towards capital adequacy

Alternatively, the moral hazard problem can be analysed with respect to banks' choice of capital under the current system of fixed-rate deposit insurance.

The ratio of capital to deposits represents another crucial indicator of the overall riskiness of bank activity. As far as capital adequacy is concerned, if a deposit insurance induces a reduction of the capital ratio, it increases the riskiness of bank. As deposit insurance reduces the depositors need to monitor bank risk-taking by increasing portfolio riskiness, it does it in respect to banks' capital choice. The moral hazard issue in terms of banks' capital adequacy arises because for the purposes of attracting and holding deposit funds, deposit insurance is a direct substitute for capital.

This distortion can be explained in the same way as the distortion in the choice of asset risk.

Let us consider a bank deciding to raise new capital.[5] In deciding how much capital to raise, the bank – as in the choice of asset risk – will act in the best interest of its present shareholders, by maximizing the total expected return on their investment without worrying about the variability of the return.

With a few modifications, Figure 3.1 can be used to illustrate the choice of capital. Let the horizontal axis now measure the amount of new capital foregone, so that a rightward movement in the diagram corresponds to a reduction in the amount of the new capital raised. The curve AA now represents the total expected return on banks' assets minus the total expected return that must be offered to investors to get them to buy the new shares. Finally, curve II continues to represent the combined expected return to the insurance agency and bank depositors. Under these conditions, the total expected return to bank shareholders equals the gap between the curves AA and II. The optimum point is again L^* where the curve AA reaches its highest value. Nevertheless, reducing the amount of new capital and moving to the right of this point decreases the expected return to the insurer, as indicated by the downward slope of II. Thus, the bank maximize the total expected return to its shareholders by raising less than the optimum amount of new capital. Hence, in the presence of deposit insurance the bank will choose a lower level of capital than it would otherwise do. The deposit insurance institution set up as an incentive for banks to limit their capital. Since insured depositors do not require bank capital to protect them against loss and the size of banks' capital account is irrelevant in attracting them, banks will be able to attract more deposits than the size of their capital can guarantee.

The analysis of banks' behaviour toward risk under a deposit insurance system showed an attitude toward increasing risk-taking. Nevertheless this attitude from bank to bank can differ in each case. In particular, Marcus (1984) points out that the bank charter value is also crucial in determining banks' optimal financial policy. By recognizing the potential loss of its valuable charter due to insolvency a bank can change its policy and assume a risk, over time as well as risk-taking behaviour. As the value of the bank charter rises the low-risk strategy is more apt to dominate whereas as the charter value falls the high-risk strategy is relatively more attractive.

Marcus argument is developed on the basis of a modified version of Merton's (1977) model.[6] Banking firms are insured and the insurer examines them each year. If the bank is insolvent, the current equity owners lose their investment and the insurer guarantees depositors against losses. At the audit, if bank assets, A, are less than B, the bank is declared insolvent and equity holders of the bank receive nothing. If $A > B$, however, the equity holders have a claim worth $A - B + C$, where C is the value of the bank charter. The charter has value if limitation on entry into the market enables banks to obtain deposits or make loans at advantageous rates. At the maturity date, T, the value of bank equity as a function of assets, A, and liabilities, B, equals

$$E(A,B,T) = 0 \qquad\qquad A < B$$

$$E(A,B,T) = A + C - B \qquad A \geq B$$

Suppose that A follows the diffusion process

$$dA = \alpha A dt + \sigma A dz$$

where
α = instantaneous expected growth rate of A;
σ = instantaneous standard deviation of the rate of return;
dz = a Weiner process

Then standard methods from the option pricing literature can be used to derive the value of equity at time 0. The time T payoff to equity holders equals max $(0, A\text{-}B)$ plus an additional payoff of C if the bank is solvent. The first term is isomorphic to a call option, and its value is well known.[7] The value of bank equity is obtained by adding the present value of the contingent payoff OC.

$$E = [AN(d_1) - e^{-rt} BN(d_2)] + e^{-rt} CN(d_2)$$

where:
r = risk-free rate of interest
d_1 = $(\log (A/B) + (r + \sigma^2/2)T)/\sigma\sqrt{T}$
d_2 = $d_1 - \sigma\sqrt{T}$
$N(.)$ = cumulative standard-normal distribution.

The term in square brackets is the value for bank equity, while the contingent claim to C has present value equal to $e^{-rt}CN(d_2)$.

Let us consider the bank's capital decision. Addition to capital increase the market value of bank equity at rate $\partial E/\partial A$ and increase current

87

owners' wealth at rate $\partial E/\partial A - 1$. Evaluating this expression we obtain:

$$N(d_1) + e^{-rT} Cn(d_2)/A\sigma\sqrt{T}) - 1 \qquad (1)$$

where n(.) is the standard normal density function.

For $C = 0$, the expression (1) reduces to $N(d_1) - 1$ which is necessarily negative; in this case, bank owners increase wealth by decreasing capital. This is the standard moral-hazard property of non risk-related deposit insurance. Nevertheless, for $C > 0$, the effect of increased capitalization on bank owners' wealth is indeterminate. Increased equity reduces the probability of default and the associated loss of the charter. For if C is large enough, this benefit dominates the reduction in the value of deposit insurance.

Marcus shows that A has a critical value A^*. If $A < A^*$ wealth is increased by lowering capital further. If $A > A^*$, value is increased by adding capital which protects the bank charter. The critical point about A^* is that it is a decreasing function of the value of the bank charter. As C falls, the low capital strategy is more likely to be chosen, since the devaluation of the charter favours the exploitation of deposit insurance.

Therefore, Marcus showed that, although in the presence of flat-premium deposit insurance a bank can transfer wealth from the insurer either by decreasing bank capital or by holding a riskier asset portfolio, banking industry is bipolar. That is a bank will choose either extreme high-risk or low-risk strategies. A priori, the moral hazard effect of deposit insurance is not determinated. However, as we will see in the next section, the possibility that deposit insurance banks to assume an excessive risk-taking behaviour, causes high social costs.

3.2 THE SOCIAL COSTS OF MORAL HAZARD

The argument here is that insured banks can benefit privately by undertaking risks that the society as a whole consider excessive. The loss to the society from the bank choice of excessive asset risk and, conversely, from the bank choice of lower ratio of capital to deposits, is clearly shown in Figure 3.1 by the difference between L and L^*. In terms of assets the shift from L^* to L represents the shift in portfolio composition toward borrowers with less productive investment projects.

In terms of capital adequacy L^* represents the socially optimum amount of new capital, and L represents a suboptimal amount of capital. The private optimal choice of banks, therefore, differs from the socially optimal choice. Ceteris paribus, in absence of deposit insurance, banks would achieve the optimal, equilibrium for society by achieving their optimal equilibrium. That is L and L^* would coincide. Allocation of resources would be optimal.

The relationship between bank private choices and the social levels of wealth is illustrated in Figures 3.3 and 3.4. Let us initially assume that all markets work perfectly, there are no problems of market power, externalities, income distribution inequities, information asymmetries. We also assume that all members of society are risk-neutral. In this framework, bank shareholders operate within the domain of unlimited liability. If the bank fails, its owners loose their investment and must repay depositors.[8]

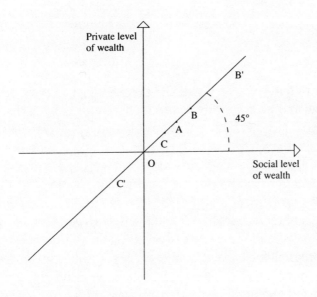

Figure 3.3: Unlimited liabilities

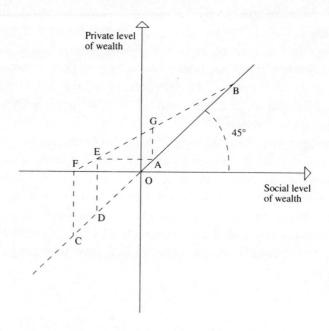

Figure 3.4: Limited liabilities

The horizontal axis of Figure 3.3 portrays social levels of wealth and the vertical axis portrays private levels of wealth – a bank shareholders at a given time. Negative values of these variables are considered because the analysis refers to a bank. The negative wealth is measured only with respect to a particular bank net worth. The 45-degree line maps private wealth equal to social wealth. Let us consider position *A* in the diagram, and a risky investment that provides the possibility of an equal gain or loss. They are represented by *B* and *C* respectively. If the probability of gain or loss were the same, the expected value of the investment would be zero, bringing the expected value of the post-investment position back to *A*. If the probability of gain were higher than even, the expected value of the post-investment wealth position would be north east of *A*; the investment would represent a private as well as a social gain. On the contrary if the probability of gain were lower than even the post investment wealth position would fall to southwest of *A*; the investment would represent a private and a social loss, and shareholders would not

90

be expected to undertake it. Larger possible gains and losses imply the same arguments and outcomes.

This simple model shows that unlimited liability by bank's owners yields incentives so that private wealth maximization is consistent with social wealth maximisation. Let us now consider the case in which the bank shareholders operate within the domain of limited liability. It means that a deposit insurance system stands by to repay depositors. If a bank fails, the owners' liability is limited to the value of bank net worth. Once the bank net worth is exhausted, the responsibility for the shortfall bears on the insurer. In this framework, the insurer is exposed to the moral hazard of bank shareholders.

Figure 3.4 describes such a case. The zero wealth represents the limited liability point for the bank's shareholders, and their wealth position is constrained from below at zero. Thus the locus of private-social wealth outcomes is represented by segmented line *FOB*.

Let us consider as before, a risky investment with the same size and probability of gain or loss, *B* or *C* in the diagram. In reality *C* is an arbitrary point. It represents the loss that would have occurred in a world of unlimited private liability. The expected private gain from the investment is represented by point *G*, and bank shareholders would undertake it. The locus of private gains from all possible odds on investment is represented by the line *FB*. As can be seen, the probability could decline far below $\frac{1}{2} = \frac{1}{2}$, such that the expected value of the investment is negative and the expected post-investment social wealth position falls as far as *D* which has the same characteristic of *C*. Since *E* represents the same expected private wealth level as starting point *A*, shareholders would still undertake the investment.

Thus, shareholders are able to undertake riskier investment, facing an unchanged expected value. The insurer is thus likely to be exposed to an excessive risk-taking by shareholders. It is not profitable for the insurer and the society. Therefore regulatory disincentives to bank excessive risk-taking need to be established in the interest of the insurer and society. The introduction of one distortion — the insurance – offers are required to prevent too great a departure from the socially ideal result that an unregulated market mechanism would yield.

3.3 REGULATION AND SUPERVISION AS RESPONSES TO DEPOSIT INSURANCE

In presence of deposit insurance banks' behaviour towards excessive risk-taking prevents the achievement of an optimal allocation of resources.

The deposit insurance establishment, which is intended to mitigate the possibility of disruptive bank runs, removes deposit discipline on banks' behaviour. The increased banks' attitude toward risk then requires additional constraints on bank activity. Therefore, improving financial stability by deposit insurance requires the achievement of opposite equilibriums.

By using a simple diagram we can illustrate the scope for bank regulation in terms of social optimum. Every bank is represented by a point in Figure 3.5. Banks' socially optimal degree of asset risk (or socially optimal amount of new capital) is represented on the horizontal axis. Each point on the axis corresponds to different L^* in Figure 3.1. Banks' preferred amount of asset risk (or capital level) is represented on vertical axis. Each point corresponds to different L in Figure 3.1. At least every bank will choose the socially optimal degree of risk. Thus, all banks will fall in the area above the 45-degree line, where $L \geq L^*$.

The main effect of bank regulation can be viewed as imposing an upper limit on banks' risk-taking. In the diagram this limit is . To the extent that regulation is effective, it will tend to alleviate the moral hazard problem by forcing banks in area K to reduce their risk-taking closer to the socially optimum level. Given that the upper limit is enforced, however, banks falling in the area below K, H, will not be affected at all by regulation, and banks falling in the area Z – whose socially optimal degree of risk is relatively high – will be forced to reduce their risk-taking below the socially optimal level. Therefore regulation implies distortive effects on banks' behaviour because the socially optimal level of risk differs across banks.

Notwithstanding these issues on the effectiveness of banks' risk-taking limits, experience shows that the introduction of deposit insurance has typically been accompanied by regulation to counteract its distortive effects and to make society better off.

One way risk-taking has been curbed is through explicit limits on the types of loans and investments banks can make. Banks are subject to a

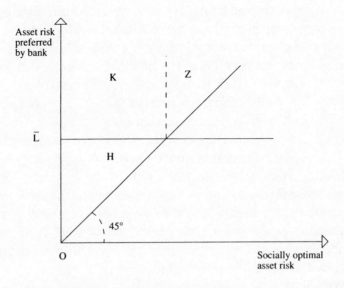

Figure 3.5: Effect of regulation on bank risk-taking

large number of restrictions on the type or quality of assets they may hold in their portfolio. Banks cannot own stocks or significant amounts of real estate. They are prohibited from investing more than a specified percentage of their capital in loans to the same borrower. Also banks can face restrictions on the margin loans for the purchase of securities.

The second mechanism to limit risk-taking is bank capital requirements. Capital requirements reduce the incentive of owners to increase risk since a greater amount of capital involves a larger loss for the owners in the event of failure. Furthermore, a bank whose acquisition of risky assets is blocked by portfolio regulation could increase its shareholders' expected return by lowering its equity cushion. By imposing minimum net worth the limited owners liability effect is curbed (see paragraph 3.2).

Interest rate ceilings can represent another form of regulation. They limit the bank competition for selected types of deposit funds. Interest rate ceilings prevent banks from funding their excessive risk-taking by simply paying a modest premium over the market interest rate. Since deposit insurance, depositors are indifferent to the riskiness of investments, thus higher interest rates attract larger funds.

Finally, regulation on banks' risk-taking can be provided by limiting bank holding companies to activity closely related to banking.

All these regulatory mechanisms do not arise only because of deposit insurance. They are peculiar to the financial environment and deposit insurance gives rise to their increase and improvement.

Supervision, on the contrary, is peculiar to regulatory policy associated with the deposit insurance establishment.

This kind of regulation has a purpose similar to the covenants that are found in virtually every debt contract: to prevent bank management from undertaking activities that increase risk to the detriment of existing creditors or the insurance funds. Through regulatory supervision, in fact, the insuring agency tries to limit the amount of risk a bank can take.

Insurance agency supervision, could be viewed as the insurance implicit premium. As far as supervision interferes with insured institution operations, then it represents an indirect cost of insurance which is added to its explicit cost, the premium.

Regulation and supervision are similar with respect to their target to limit bank risky behaviour. Nevertheless, since the latter is a special mechanism associated with insurer activity, their effectiveness is different. As Buser, Chen and Kane (1981) have pointed out, besides selling deposit guarantee, at bargain explicit rates, deposit insurance[9] performs four regulatory functions:

1. Entry regulation; new banks entering the insurance system are accurately examined;
2. Periodical examination; banks' records are inspected and managerial activity supervised regularly;
3. Regulation of deposit rates and withdrawal; deposit insurance has extensive rules of applicability;
4. Disposition of failed banks; when an insured bank fails, the insurer usually chooses whether and how to liquidate it.

The described supervisory activity is, on the whole, intended to control the banks capital adequacy to acceptable standards.[10] In particular, regulation and periodic examination of individual banks balance sheet ratios function together to maintain charter value and to control the moral hazard inherent in the deposit insurance activity.

To analyse the implicit dimension of deposit insurance – supervision – let us consider a bank operating without insurance guarantee. In Figure 3.6 the value of this bank is represented under the condition of costly bankruptcy, where consequently, increasing leverage offsets the growing incentive to expand debt (deposits). The value of the bank is maximized at V_0 and $D_0 - D^{max}$ represents the point of zero equity, where debt-capital by itself is sufficient to finance the bank's entire portfolio. V_u denotes the value of the bank in an unlevered state.

Now imagine the introduction of a governmental agency which guarantees bank deposits. We assume for simplicity that the insurance coverage extends to all deposit balances and that it is offered without charge. Neither explicit fees nor regulatory interference therefore exist. The V_I curve portrays the value of the bank with free insurance. The vertical distance between V_I and V represents the value of free insurance as assessed by the bank. When insurance fees are set according to this "distance", the with-insurance value of the bank, net of the explicit insurance premium, would coincide with its uninsured value for each level of deposits (curve V).

The insurer strategy – according to the reality – is to set a flat premium, and to establish regulatory devices to control excess demand for insurance services. The insurer thus offers a bank at least one opportunity to increase its value above the maximal value as an insured bank. In Figure 3.6 the boundary for bank indifference to deposit insurance is the horizontal line V_0V_0. At the same time, maximum feasible increases in value are given by V_I, the locus of firm value under free insurance. To limit the opportunity set, let us suppose that the insurer introduces such incentives to prevent the insured bank from increasing its deposit leverage beyond the level D^F. Thus, the triangle ABC represents the locus of mutually acceptable contracting opportunities.

Periodically, the insurer appraises the economic value of the bank's assets and liabilities. The residual capital position is then compared to the agency's standard for capital adequacy, which may be unique for each bank. The model assumes that the standard is known to bank in advance of the examination date.

Let us suppose that agency bank examinations place the bank into one of the three set basic states. The three states are shown in Figure 3.7 in relation to the probability distribution for bank's capital value on the next examination date, conditional on the bank's current portfolio. In state I,

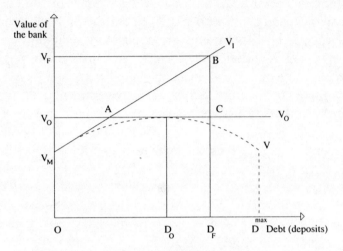

Figure 3.6: Limits on acceptable insurance contracting

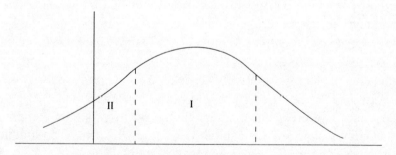

Figure 3.7: Probability distribution for bank capital
(conditional on bank's current portfolio)

96

bank's capital is judged to be adequate, and according to the model, the bank is presumed to pose no moral hazard. In state II bank's capital is inadequate. Nevertheless, the bank is asked to strengthen asset and liability portfolio to reduce its need for capital under the agency adequacy norms, and it is allowed to operate.[11] In state III, the extent of capital deficiency is such that the agency must declare the bank technically insolvent. The boundary between the second and third state cannot be strictly shown in the diagram because usually the agency assists the bank to avoid its book value of stockholder equity becoming zero. By assuming that the insolvency declaration occurs only when the market value of bank's portfolio and its physical assets falls seriously below that of its deposit liabilities, the state II can be bounded at some positive fraction of the value of the bank's charter to continue in operation.

The agencys regulatory interference operates as restricting the set of profit opportunities that an affected bank may exploit in states II and III. Let us assume direct supervision interference result in a reduction in bank value, at state II, and in bank closure at state III, with the residual value of its lost charter serving as the bank's cost of bankruptcy. This regulatory structure is aimed to reduce the bank's incentive to substitute deposit debt for capital, that, occurs in the presence of deposit insurance. Since in this agency regulatory framework, increased leverage increases the expected costs of being discovered either to be insolvent, or to have inadequate capital, the bank will adjust its capital value at least prior of each examination.

The regulatory interference effects of the insuring agency are shown in Figure 3.8. The curve V_I, as in Figure 3.6, shows the locus of firm value under free insurance. The introduction of supervision activities, causes, for every positive value of debt, the value of insured bank to be reduced by corresponding deadweight losses. Thus the curve V_{IR} indicates the with-regulation value of bank, net of the explicit insurance premium. The vertical distance between the V_I and V_{IR} curves represents the varying value of implicit insurance premiums, which is the implicit insurance cost, due to the contingent supervision interference accepted as a condition for insurance. The curve V, which portrays the value of the bank without any insurance, is displayed in the diagram as well. Therefore, the figure allows to measure the net benefit to the bank from exchanging insurance agency's regulation for potential losses from costly

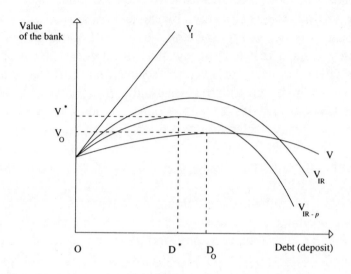

Figure 3.8: The impact of surveillance on the value of an insured bank

bankruptcy. This benefit is favourable to the bank at a low deposit level, but it becomes unfavourable at high deposit levels.

The final step is to introduce in the model the explicit premium for the insurance. The premium is assumed fixed per unit of deposits. Thus value of the insured bank, in presence of implicit and explicit premium, is portrayed by the curve V_{IR-p}. It represents the curve V_{IR} reduced by the appropriate constant fraction (p) of deposit levels.

Now, the optimal level of insured deposit with explicit and implicit insurance costs is denoted by D^*. The corresponding point V^*, on the curve V_{IR-p} is the optimum bank value. On the other hand $D_0 V_0$ denotes the optimum bank value without insurance.

This model provides a descriptive framework to analyse the explicit as well as the implicit cost of deposit insurance, whereas the implicit dimensions of the insurance agency pricing strategy convert the explicit premium into a convenient device to adjust the net insurance subsidy that any insurance system finances from tax-exempt earnings on its fund.

Therefore in this model, insurers' regulation and supervision activities on bank behaviour cannot be disaggregated from its guarantee activity.

Although from a different point of view Merton (1978) investigated the double dimension of deposit insurance costs. Merton's model provides a formal setting for evaluating the cost of deposit insurance that explicitly takes into account surveillance or auditing costs and provides for random auditing times.[12] The insuring agency (expressly the Fdic) when insures bank debts – deposits – receives a premium and it is assumed to face a liability of actual and potential cash outflows for surveillance costs and for any shortfall between assets and depositors in the event of the bank's liquidation. Therefore, insurance agency liability has two sources: the guarantee of deposits and the surveillance and audit cost. The former is demonstrated to be a monotonically decreasing function of the asset-to-deposit ratio, the latter, on the contrary, is a monotonically increasing function of the same ratio. Furthermore the bank equity per unit of deposit is a monotonically increasing function of the asset-to-deposit ratio. In this framework and under the assumption of free entry, into the banking industry, the equilibrium interest rate on deposit is derived. This equilibrium rate of return on deposit results to be below the market interest rate. The spread between the two rates exactly equal the expected auditing cost per deposit per unit time. Merton concludes that, in fact, depositors pay for the cost of surveillance and the bank's equity holders pay for the deposit guarantee.

These analyses have pointed out the special features of deposit insurance as an intervention in the financial market. The trade off between its positive effects on the banking industry stability and its perverse effects on the banks behaviour towards risk, arises the case for a special banks regulation. The supervision and surveillance performed by insurance agency together with the guarantee role are the main aspect of this special regulation, which provides additional costs to banks' activity.

3.4 IMPLICIT INSURANCE

The actual deposit insurance handling of banks' crises represents an additional issue about its performance.

If the deposit insurance schemes were actually insurance-based, their intervention would be requested and justified at the occurrence of losses to depositors from a bank failure. Since most of the existing insuring agencies – the Fdic first of all – are entitled to declare a bank legally insolvent, in fact, they set the burdens and the terms of their intervention. Furthermore, under the existing deposit insurance rules of applicability, a technically insolvent bank does not necessarily need to be liquidated.

The evolution of Fdic options in handling failure represents a useful phenomenon to investigate. Insofar as the Fdic's intervention departs from a typical insurance intervention, the analysis of its experience becomes extendible to other deposit protection schemes.

When a bank approaches a failure, several procedures can be employed for dealing with the situation. The most straightforward action is the deposit payoff. Insured depositors received payments up to the insurance limit if it exists. Other depositors – uninsured and depositors with accounts over the insurance limit, become general creditors of the failed bank and they receive payments if collections on assets exceed liabilities. A payoff procedure therefore, imposed losses on uninsured creditors unless the liquidation generates sufficient cash to meet the obligations. Furthermore, banking services are temporarily disrupted.

As an alternative to payoff and liquidation, an acquisition of the failed bank by another institution can be arranged. In this transaction, all of the failed bank's deposit liabilities are assumed by the acquiring bank, which also purchase some of the failed bank's assets. This procedure is often preferred to the payoff because it has several economic advantages. Intangible assets are made safe and the going-concern value of the failed bank is preserved. Nevertheless, this procedure, disrupts the market discipline by uninsured depositors of the risks assumed by banks. If uninsured depositors believe that they will always be protected by a P&A, they have no reason to exercise care in selection of their bank.

A third procedure has been adopted by the Fdic, since 1983. It is aimed at combining the economies of the P&A with the discipline-encouraging aspects of the payoff. With a modified payoff, it is arranged for another bank to assume only the insured deposits of a failed bank. Uninsured depositors receive an immediate credit for the amount of their claims that the Fdic estimates will ultimately be recovered. The acquiring bank pays a premium, which reduces losses, and the acquired bank generally remains open.

Finally, under certain circumstances the agency makes loans to failing banks or purchases assets from them, that is direct assistance is provided. The major criticism of the use of this option is that it may be a means to bail out stockholders. When a bank is declared insolvent its stockholders lose their entire investment, whereas stockholders in banks that received direct assistance suffered substantial but not total loss.

The insuring agency's policy – Fdic or others' – of handling bankruptcy is not without implication for banks' preference for risky or safe financial structure and then for the banking system as a whole. The argument is that increasing use of procedures involving implicit insurance for all of the failed bank's deposits, increases the banks preference for a high risk strategy as well. The "too large to fail" or "too large to allow depositors to suffer loss" policies adopted in practice by deposit insurance systems, thereby their ongoing practices, are an additional circumstance that affects the allocation of resources and competition in banking.

The perverse effects of implicit insurance on bank's portfolio choices have been rigorously considered by Penati and Protopapadakis (1986), by constructing a model of banks' behaviour under the current insurance systems.

In the model banks operate in two separate markets: each bank makes loans in its local market and all banks make loans (z-loans) in another market in competition with other banks and with nonbank lenders. This assumption about the two markets enable us to describe a banking system in which banks share a common risk, but they also carry risks that are specific to each bank.[14] Therefore, it is this characteristic of local loans that differentiates banks in the model.

The banking environment described by the model assumes the existence of a local monopoly and a competitive z-loans market. Thus, each bank faces a downward sloping demand curve for loans in its local market and each bank is a price-taker with respect to the z-loan rate. Furthermore the model assumes that banks offer both insured deposits, for which they pay a risk free rate (flat-premium) and deposits that are not insured contractually for which they have to pay appropriate rates of return.[15] Also, banks' equity is fixed and banks expand at margin by obtaining insured and uninsured deposits in fixed proportions. In this settlement the Jth bank is assumed to maximize the present value of its profits. The maximization problem is given by:

$$\underset{r_{lj},Z_J}{\text{MAX}} \; P_J \;=\; \delta(1-\pi_z)(1-\pi_l) \; \{Z_j(1+r_z)+L_j(1+r_{lj})$$

$$-(V_J \bar{E}_J) \; [d_i(1+r_f)+d_u(1+r_{uj})]\} \;=\; P_J \qquad (1)$$

where:

P_J	=	present value of bank's profits
$(1-\pi_z)$	=	probability of good state for z-loan,
π_z	=	probability of z-loan's default;
$(1-\pi_l)$	=	probability of good state for local loan;
π_l	=	probability of local loan's default;
Z_j	=	the Jth bank's z-loans in the 1st period;
L_j	=	the Jth bank's local loans in the 1st period;
r_z	=	z-loans rate (it is given by the market);
r_{lj}	=	local loans interest rate chosen by Jth bank;
V_J	=	the Jth bank's value of all deposits plus equity;
$\bar{E}_J$	=	the Jth bank's fixed amount of equity;
r_f	=	risk-free rate;
r_{uJ}	=	the Jth bank's rate on uninsured deposits
d_i	=	fraction of insured deposits
d_u	=	fraction of uninsured deposits
δ	=	constant of proportionality of the state prices.

Thus, $\delta(1-\pi_z)(1-\pi_l)$ are the state prices, which are proportional to the probability of each state and where $\delta = 1/1 + r_f$ for assumption. $Z_j(1+r_z)+L_j(1+r_{lj})$ is the Jth bank cash flow outcome at the 2nd period and $(V_J \bar{E}_J)$ is the value of all deposits, insured and uninsured.[16] Finally, $[d_i(1+r_f)+d_u(1+r_{uj})]$ is the cost of deposits, insured and uninsured. Therefore, the expression in curly brackets is the value of Jth bank's equity. The model assumes, for simplicity that the insurance premium is equal to zero, and that there are no bankruptcy costs.

The equilibrium values of (1) are subject to:

$$Z_J \geq 0, \quad L_J > 0 \qquad (a)$$

$$\frac{P_J}{E_J} \geq \frac{(1+r_t)}{(1-\pi_z)(1-\pi_l)} \qquad (b)$$

and

$$1+r_{uj} = \gamma \qquad (c)$$

where the term on the right of (b) is the competitive market return paid for the risk incurred by equity-holders, and γ is the cost of uninsured deposits.[17]

The first-order condition for the local loans is:

$$1 + r_{IJ} = \frac{L_J}{L_J} + \frac{(1 + r_t)}{(1 - \pi_l)} \phi_l \tag{2}$$

where

$$\phi_l = \frac{d_i(1 - \pi_z)(1 - \pi_l) + d_u}{1 - \pi_z d_i}$$

Thus the return on local loans depends on the risk free rate and the probability of no default in that local loan. Furthermore it depends on the elasticity of the demand for local borrowing and, finally, on the explicit deposit insurance on r_{IJ}. The element ϕ_l measures this effect.

Considering the assumption of perfect competition in z-loans market the rate charged to z-loans is:[18]

$$1 + r_{IJ} = \frac{(1 + r_t)}{(1 - \pi_l)} \phi_z \tag{3}$$

where

$$\phi_z = \frac{d_i(1 - \pi_z)(1 - \pi_l) + d_u}{1 - \pi_l d_i}$$

Again ϕ_z captures the effect of insurance on the z-loan pricing decision.

If there is no insurance ($d_i = 0$), then $\phi_z = 1$, that is banks price z-loans exactly as the competitive capital market. The existence of explicit deposit insurance results in $\phi_z < 1$, and z-loans are made by banks exclusively at rates subsidized by the insurance. Furthermore, since $\phi_l < 1$, the insurance subsidize also local loans.[19] Hence, the model shows that deposit insurance provides a subsidy for loans.

A second important result of the model is that the insurance subsidy increases with risk. Differentiating ϕ_z and ϕ_l with respect to π_z and π_l, the values of the derivates are:[20]

$$\frac{\delta\phi_z}{\delta\pi_z} < 0 \ ; \quad \frac{\delta\phi_z}{\delta\pi_l} > 0$$

and similarly

$$\frac{\delta\phi_l}{\delta\pi_l} < 0 \ ; \quad \frac{\delta\phi_l}{\delta\pi_z} > 0$$

These results show that not only the subsidy increases with risk, but also that it declines as the risk of other loans increases.

The model can be used now to investigate the effect of the implicit insurance on banks' pricing risk, by assuming that the deposit insurance enlarges its intervention to uninsured deposits as well, if a given proportion of banks fail, namely α. This assumption is consistent with the actual strategy of deposit insurance schemes. In particular, in Penati and Protopapadakis' setting, the insurance scheme provides implicit insurance to contractually uninsured deposits when failures occur in such a size to threaten the financial system stability. Because of the previous assumptions about the nature of the markets where banks operate, z-loans now become the crucial variable. Since the z-loan market is assumed competitive and all banks compete with each other, banks share a common risk. Therefore if z-loans fail, then all the banks fail: z-loans become a systemic risk. In this case the insurance will protect uninsured depositors regardless the set value of α.

Let us consider that z-loans do not fail. The probability that the representative bank will fail is π_l, and $1 - \pi_l$ that it will not. These probabilities are independent across banks and, hence, the distribution of failures is binomial and independent of the individual bank decisions. The deposit insurance will intervene to protect uninsured depositors according with the probability determined by the decision on α; labelled by $1 - \sigma$. The probability of uninsured depositors not being paid in full is given by:

$$\pi_n = \sigma\,\pi_l(1 - \pi_z)$$

As before, the z-loan rate and the local rate can be determined by maximizing the net value of profits. Thus:

$$1 + \hat{r}_z = 1 + r_f$$

and

$$1 + \hat{r}_l = -\frac{L}{L'} + \frac{1 + r_t}{1 - \pi_l}\ \hat{\phi}_l$$

where $\hat{r}_z$ =   z-loans rate with implicit insurance;

         $\hat{r}_l$ =   local loans rate with implicit insurance;

Furthermore:

$$\hat{\phi}_z = 1 - \pi_z$$

and

$$\phi_l = \frac{d_i(1 - \pi_l)(1 - \pi_n) + d_u((1 - \pi_l)}{1 - \pi_n}$$

These relations imply that $\hat{\phi}_z < \phi_z$ and $\hat{r}_z < r_z$. This means that implicit deposit insurance increases the insurance subsidy to z-loans and lowers the rate banks charge for them. Similarly could be derivated that implicit deposit insurance also increases the insurance subsidy to local loans, but not necessarily reduces their interest rate.

In conclusion, the existing implicit insurance, inherent to the long-standing practices of deposit insurance schemes, has distortive effects on banks' portfolio choices. Deposit insurance, in general, subsidizes risky loans; the presence of an implicit guarantee on contractually uninsured deposits makes this distortion worse. The model, in particular, by assuming the division of banks' market in two separate and different segment, makes meaningful the distinction between explicit and implicit deposit insurance.

Also Pennacchi (1978) has shown the impact of deposit insurance policy strategies on banks' incentive for risk-taking. By expanding a model of deposit insurance pricing and bank equity valuation a setting is derived to analyse questions concerning banks' behaviour under alternative policy regimes. In particular, under the assumption of a merger policy (P&A) of handling bank failures, associated to the assumption of

105

an agency charging a fair premium, for deposit insurance, banks result preferring a high risk strategy, that is a greater leverage. On the contrary for the case of direct payment to insured depositors, banks prefer greater capital, less leverage. Furthermore if monopoly rents exist, in the case of P & A transaction, banks will always prefer less capital regardless of the size of their monopoly rents, whereas in the case of direct payments sufficient monopoly rents will induce banks to prefer greater capital.

Therefore, evidence arises that the actual handling strategy of deposit insurance schemes, regardless their statute or formal characteristics, are crucial in determining their final impact on the banking industry. As far as deposit insurance departs from its insurance nature, banks' behaviour departs from competitive and efficiency criteria.

NOTES

1. Flannery (1982) and Murton (1989).
2. Keeton (1984).
3. The return on bank assets is net of any bankruptcy costs, because they use up part of bank's assets.
4. $P_2 = \mu R/r$
5. In this attempt we shall concentrate on the flow of new capital into banking rather than on the capital stock.
6. Merton (1977) developed a model of the cost for deposit insurance by the application of option pricing theory.
7. Smith (1976).
8. Following the approach of White (1989).
9. They refer expressly to Fdic. However the analysis could be employed to illustrate the deposit insurance suspension activity in general.
10. Currently, banks are required to maintain a minimum of 5.5 per cent primary capital relative to bank assets (Murton, 1989).
11. Alternatively, the bank might be asked to make up some of equity deficiency by raising new capital or restricting current and subsequent dividend payments.
12. The method used to derive this evaluation setting exploits the isomorphic correspondence between loan guarantees and common stock put options. This correspondence has been demonstrated by Merton in an earlier paper (1977).
13. On the market discipline by uninsured depositors see Baer and Brewer (1986). Using US banks' data from 1974 to 1982, they found a strong responsiveness of CD (Certificates of Deposits) holders behaviour to difference in bank risk. Furthermore they found that the sensitivity of uninsured deposit rates to change in risk variables diminishes the relevance of deposit insurance systems. Therefore, a strengthening of implicit guarantee for uninsured deposits could eliminate an important source of market discipline.

14. From the point of view of the banking system, local loans become idiosyncratic risk and the others loans are systemic risk.

15. This assumption implies that the representative bank chooses the interest rate it charge for its local loans (r_l), while it takes the loan rate for z-loan (r_z). Furthermore, since insured deposits pay off in all states – good or bankruptcy – the bank needs to offer only the risk-free rate (r_f) to attract such deposits, while the bank has to pay.

16. The value of insured deposits is $(V_J - E_J)d_i$ and the value of uninsured deposits is $(V_J - E_J)d_u$.

17.
$$\tau = \frac{1 + r_t}{(1 - \pi_z)(1 - \pi_l)} - \frac{\pi_l}{1 - \pi_l} \cdot \frac{z_j}{(V_J - E_J)} (1 + r_l) -$$

$$- \frac{\pi_z}{1 - \pi_l} \frac{L_J}{(V_J - E_J)} (1 + r_U)$$

18. Each bank takes the prevailing z-loan rate. thus, the amount of Jth bank's lending can be found by equating its marginal cost of lending to its marginal revenue $(1 + r_z)$.

19. $\phi < 1$, that $d_i(1 - \pi_z)(1 - \pi_l) + d_u < 1 - \pi_f d_i$. Since $d_i + d_u = 1$, then $-\pi_z d_i(1 - \pi_l) < 0$, which shows that $\phi_z < 1$ always. Similarly for ϕ_l results $-\pi_f d_i(1 - \pi_l) < 1$.

20.
$$\frac{\delta\phi_z}{\delta\pi_z} = \frac{d_i(1 - \pi_l)}{d_i(1 - \pi_f d_i)} < 0 \; ;$$

$$\frac{\delta\phi_z}{\delta\pi_l} = \frac{d_i(1 - \pi_z)}{1 - \pi_f d_i} \left[\frac{d_i + d_u / (1 - \pi_z) - \pi_f d_i}{1 - \pi_f d_i} \right] > 1$$

4 Coping with deposit insurance perverse effects

Deposit insurance, while successful in eliminating widespread panics, has built-in risk-taking incentives that may serve to exacerbate any tendency toward banking instability.

There is a paradox inherent in deposit insurance. By making banks safer for individual depositors, the banking system as a whole has been made less safe because of current deposit insurance pricing procedures and because of its bank insolvency handling.

In absence of deposit insurance, riskier banks will be able to attract deposits only at higher rates and these higher costs of funding serve as built-in market regulated incentives to limit excessive risk-taking by banks. As introduction of deposit insurance makes deposits equally risk-free across banks, these incentives disappear and regulation and close supervision of the banking industry – as we have seen – must necessarily replace them as deterrents to excessive risk-taking. This means that a trade-off exists between the benefits of financial stability and the costs of possible misallocation of resources associated with excessive risk-taking.

To maintain positive effects on financial stability provided by deposit insurance and to mitigate its perverse effects on bank behaviour and on the system in general – also because of regulation and supervision – many reform proposals have been considered by economists and monetary authorities. The proposals' common aim is twofold: to reduce banks excessive risk-taking and to reduce insurer's uncompensated liability from guaranteeing deposits.

The proposals range in scope from changes in deposit insurance pricing, in capital requirements to a complete overhaul of the thrift industry's regulatory structure. Each different option for reform depends on the different view of deposit insurance problems. A microeconomic view focuses on deposit insurance as an actuarially working system; a wider prospective considers both the financial and the real sector issues. Thus critics of banking regulation arguing for a reform of deposit insurance stress the need to enhance market discipline and to reduce reliance on regulatory discretion in closing insolvent institutions.

Finally some approaches are more radical in that they postulate either restriction on the use to which insured deposits are put or the displacement of government deposit insurance with private deposit insurance.

4.1 OPTIMAL DEPOSIT INSURANCE DESIGN

A socially optimal deposit insurance scheme should seek to reduce the probability of bank panics while minimizing any resources misallocation costs resulting from the supply of that insurance.

Many critics of the present deposit protection system have long advocated risk-sensitive deposit insurance premiums as the correct response to the perverse risk incentive of insured banks. According to these critics changing insurance premiums that appropriately rise with the risk undertaken by a given institution, would have the advantage of allowing that institution to pay a fair price to the insuring agency for the level of risk it chooses. This argument is based on an actuarially prospective of deposit insurance. As far as the insurance premium reflects the probability of bank failure, depending on the risk of bank activities, it is the right price for protection and it represents an efficient disincentive for banks to gamble.

Deposit insurance schemes have historically set premiums irrespective of a banking institution's potential liability to the insurer agency so that low-risk institutions may have been overcharged for deposit protection while other high-risk institutions may have been undercharged.

Deposit insurance rates that vary with the riskiness of an institution's assets and liabilities have been suggested by many as a preferable means of dealing with deposit insurance problems. Premium is hence considered the key variable to balance risk and protection from depositor point of view. Furthermore the premium balances the risk and its coverage from the insurance agency point of view, so that premium balances fairly social costs and benefits.

In terms of the expression written in the first chapter the single bank premium providing the optimal insurance scheme would be:

$$p_i = l_i(\theta_i) + C_i(\gamma_i) + e_i \qquad (1)$$

where the right part of the expression considers the expected insurer loss associated with the ith bank failure within the premium setting period l_i, depending on a vector (θ_i) of risk of the i bank, the cost function $C_i(\gamma_i)$ reflecting the insurer monitoring, surveillance and auditing costs and, finally, some social cost adjustment to the private cost of insurance provision to account for externalities, e_i.

The expression above describes a first-best pricing scheme that can be compared with the current pricing scheme:

$$p_i = kD_i \qquad (2)$$

as a constant amount of deposits, irrespective of risk characteristics of banks.

Risk-sensitive premium supporters argue that a properly constructed price schedule for insurance would reduce the spread between scheme (1) and (2) with evident social and private benefits. Moreover a fair insurance premium as that of (1) could enhance bank discipline because it would impose a direct economic incentive for banks to limit their risk-taking activities and any public disclosure of the premium paid by a bank, could trigger additional market responses based on a revision of perceived risk levels.[1] The proper measurement of risk would in theory allow the complete dismantling of all existing regulation and capital standard.

However the main objective of a risk-related insurance premiums is to introduce price mechanism into the insurance system so that each institution takes risk until the marginal cost of risk – measured by the insurance premium – is equal to the marginal benefit – measured by the rate of return on the investment. A correctly set premium would induce the optimal degree of risk-taking as for every other type of insurance.

This idea of introducing price mechanism effectiveness in deposit insurance is quite appealing, nevertheless, it is not straightforward to derive a formula for a fair insurance premium which considers banks' risk exposure.

The next section outlines a theoretic derivation for deposit insurance pricing which has suggested a particularly convenient way to take bank assets and liabilities structure and assets quality into account.

4.1.1 Pricing risk-adjusted deposit insurance

A seminal approach to the determination of the appropriate insurance premium has been offered by Merton (1977), who applied the Black-Scholes (1973) option pricing framework to the analysis of deposit insurance. In particular, Merton has shown that when an insurance agency examines a bank at specific intervals, demand-deposit guarantees are analogous to put option and can be valued using standard option-pricing techniques.

The periodic inspections by the banking agency, in effect, make bank deposits similar to debt claims with an effective maturity equal to the examination interval and then an isomorphic relationship between deposit insurance and common stock put option exists.

Merton's starting point is the observation that an efficient way to save large information and surveillance costs on banks for depositors, small depositors in particular, is to have third-party guarantee deposits whereas the capability and willingness of that part to meet its obligation are beyond question. The key question is hence to determine the costs on the guarantor.

Merton's focus on insurance pricing arises from considering insurance agency costs for the guarantee it offers on deposits.

According to a put option on a common stock the owner of given shares has the right to sell a specified number of them at a specified price per share on a specified date. The put owner in this contract has a choice whether or not to exercise his option to sell at the specified price. If the option is not exercised on the expiration date, the contract expires and is worthless. If on the expiration date the stock price per share is higher than the exercise price per share, that is $p_S > p_E$, the put owner would clearly not exercise his right to sell the stock at p_E when he could sell it at

111

p_S on the open market. Hence if $p_S > p_E$ the put will be allowed to expire. If, on the contrary, on the expiration date $p_S < p_E$, then the put owner will exercise his right and the value of the put option will be $(p_E - p_S)$ for each share. The value of put option on one share of stock at the expiration date is then:

$$P(0) = \text{Max} \, [\, 0, p_E - p_S \,] \tag{3}$$

where $P(t)$ is the price of a put with length of time T to go before expiration.

Let us now consider the case of deposit insurance which guarantees a bank's promise to pay to its lenders a total of B units of money on a specific date – the maturity date – always, even if bank assets V are less than the value of bank debt B. Then on the maturity date the value of equity is Max $[0, V - B]$; the value of guarantor's claim is Min $[0, V - B]$ and the value of debt is always B because it is riskless. As Merton points out the presence of the guarantor creates an additional cash inflow to the bank of $-\text{Min} \, [0, V - B]$ units of money, or conversely of Max $[0, B - V]$.

If $G(T)$ is the value to the firm of the guarantee when length of time until the maturity date of deposits is T, then

$$G(0) = \text{Max} \, [0, B - V] \tag{4}$$

From this result arises that the properties of deposit insurance are isomorphic to those of a put option, in fact (3) and (4) are identical: B corresponds to p_E, the exercise price, and V corresponds to p_S. By granting deposit insurance coverage, the insuring agency writes a put and becomes the true bearer of the bank's downside asset value risk.

To derive the formula of the value of guarantee we can consider the value of the put. At the expiration date the value of the put depends on V and its value prior to the expiration will depend on the probability distribution for the range of assets on the expiration date. By assuming that bank assets follow a diffusion process with long-normal return, that is a constant variance per unit time, and using the frictionless market assumption the formula is:

$$G(T) = B_c^{-rT} \phi \, (x_2) - v \phi \, (x_1) \tag{5}$$

where:

$$x_i \equiv [\log(B/V) - \left(r + \frac{s^2}{2}T\right)] / \sigma\sqrt{T} \; ;$$

$$x_2 \equiv x_2 + \sigma\sqrt{T} \; ;$$

and

$\phi(\cdot)$ = cumulative density function;
V = current value of bank's assets;
r = market rate of interest on riskless securities for unit time;
σ^2 = variable rate per unit time for the logarithmic changes in the value of assets.

This equation can be used to evaluate the cost to the insurer of using deposit with a face value of B units of money and maturity T. Insured depositors are riskless and their current value can be written as:[2]

$$D = B_c^{-rT}$$

Then the cost of the guarantee per unit of insured deposits, that is $G(T)/D$ can be written as a function of two variables $d \equiv D/V$ – the current deposit-to-asset value ratio – and $t \equiv \sigma^2 T$ – the variance of the logarithmic change in the value of the assets during the term of the deposits:[3]

$$g(d,T) = \phi(h_2) - \frac{1}{d}\phi(h_1) \qquad (6)$$

where

$$h_1 \equiv \log(d) - \frac{\tau}{2} \Big/ \sqrt{T}$$

$$h_2 \equiv h_1 + \sqrt{T}$$

Form equation (6) two consequences derive. The first:

$$\frac{\partial g}{\partial d} = \phi(h_1)/d \qquad (6')$$

that is, the change in the cost with respect to an increase in the D/V is positive. The second consequence is:

113

$$\frac{\partial g}{\partial \tau} = \phi(h_1)/(2d\sqrt{T}) \qquad (6'')$$

that is, the change in the cost respect to an increase in $\sigma^2\, T$ is also positive. Furthermore, as long as deposit-to-asset value ratio and the volatility of the underlying assets remain fixed, the cost of deposit insurance per unit of deposit is constant.

Finally it is important to notice that in this model the cost of deposit insurance is not affected by changes in the market rate of interest unless such changes affect d.

Hence, Merton's model, using the analogous relation between deposit guarantees and put option, determines an insurance premium that according to (6') and (6") increases with leverage of the bank and increases with a deterioration in the quality of assets.

Under the current fixed-rate system the premium paid by banks for deposit insurance coverage does not reflect the fair value of the put. Thus the shareholders of high-risk and high-leverage banks obtain more net benefits from deposit insurance than those of low-risk and low-leverage banks, since as the bank's debt becomes more risky, both deposit rate demanded by insured depositors and the insurance premium charged by the insuring agency remain unchanged. The net value of the fixed-premium guarantee increases as the risk of the bank increases whereas the some value of a variable premium – as described by option-theoretic analysis above – is constant.

Empirical calculation of the proper deposit insurance premium from market data have been provided by Marcus and Shaked (1984). They used a direct application of Merton's model by estimating the equation:

$$I = B_T c^{-rT}\,[1 - N(x_2)] \ - \ c^{-\delta T}A_0\,[1 - N(x_1)] \qquad (7)$$

where:

B_T = debt obligation of a bank, that is the level to which deposits will grow if left in the bank until the next examination;

T = time until next examination;

r = risk-free rate of interest;

$N(\cdot)$ = cumulative normal distribution;

δ = dividend rate per dollar of bank assets;

A_0 = current value of the stock that pays dividend at rate ;

σ $\quad=\quad$ instantaneous standard deviation of the rate of return of A;

x_1 $\quad=\quad$ $[\log(A_0/B_T) + (r + \sigma/2 - \delta)T] / (\sigma\sqrt{T})$;

x_2 $\quad=\quad$ $x_1 + \sigma\sqrt{T}$

As in the case of the formula derived by Merton, the insight of equation (7) is that insurance gives depositors an option to sell their claims on the bank to insuring agency at price B_T. A and σ are not directly observable, so that the authors substituted for A the expression $A = D + E - I$ where $(D + E)$ is the sum of the market values of debt plus equity and it is observable and I is the value of the current fixed rate deposit insurance (Fdic insurance). The variance of the return on the bank's asset portfolio is substituted by

$$\sigma = \sigma_E \left[1 - \frac{B_T C^{-rT} N(x_1)}{C^{-ST} A_0 N(x_1)} \right] \qquad (8)$$

as an implicit solution for σ, where σ_E is the standard deviation of the rate of return on bank equity.

Furthermore equation (7) is derived under the assumption that the current insurance system insurers all deposits.

The estimation of (7) has been run on a forty bank sample that in 1980 accounted for more than 25% per cent of total U.S. domestic deposits of all commercial banks. For each bank of the sample the proper insurance premium has been estimated and Table 4.1 contains a summary of data divided by premium intervals.

The effective annual premium paid by banks to Fdic in 1980 was one-thirtieth of 1% of deposits, that is $ 333 per million. Comparing this premium with the estimated one, the former results approximately ten times the weighted average of the estimates of insurance value. Only three of the forty banks in 1980 warranted premiums in excess of the government rate. There exist two different arguments for that: either Fdic rates are too high or they are correct for the banking system as a whole and large banks in the sample subsidize small banks. Furthermore Fdic premium rate is comprehensive of administrative and operating expenses that an insurance agency working in a competitive market does not incur, but even if we add this expense to the weighted average of the value of deposit guarantee, these values still are less than one-half the effective rate of $ 333 per million. Regardless of the precise levels of the fair

Table 4.1: Empirical estimation of the proper insurance premiums

Insurance Value	Number of Cases	Frequency	Probability Density
0–1	15	0.375	0.375
1–5	11	0.275	0.688
5–10	2	0.050	0.010
10–50	4	0.100	0.003
50–100	5	0.125	0.003
100–200	1	0.025	0.0003
200–500	2	0.050	0.0002
500–2,117	0	0	0
Median insurance value		3.5	
Mean value		28.4	
Weighted average		13.8	

Notes: Insurance values are expressed as dollars per million dollars of deposits. Probability density equals frequency divided by length of interval of insurance value. Weighted average equals total of fair premiums divided by total of deposits.

Source: Marcus and Shaked (1984).

premium the estimation of the option model suggests one more important issue. Comparing the estimates over time, premiums vary with significant extent and this is largely attributable to changes in the estimated standard deviation of asset rates of return. Even if it had been possible to measure the true value of σ without error, small change in σ still would have major effects on the fair value of deposit insurance.

Merton's theoretic model and Marcus and Shaked's estimates of the proper premium for deposit insurance disregard bank regulation and surveillance usually associated with deposit insurance schemes. In particular they do not focus the insuring agency's policy of handling bankruptcy. As we have seen political choices for resolving bank failure play an important role in determining deposit insurance effects on banks' behaviour. Thus a more developed model has to consider, as well as providing a more complete basis for insurance pricing, issues concerning bank's incentive for risk-taking under alternative policy regimes.

In 1978 Merton extended his put option model taking into account explicitly surveillance or auditing costs and providing for random auditing times, while a basic development in the theory of pricing risk adjusted deposit insurance is from Ronn and Verma (1986). For arriving at empirical estimates of deposit insurance premiums from market data by using isomorphic relationship between insurance and put option, they exploited Merton's model considering Fdic's intervention policies.

Differently from Marcus and Shaked they do not focus on the question whether the flat premium which is charged by the Fdic represent a fair value of the insurance. Moreover from their point of view it is meaningless to deal with a fair premium without considering the extent of Fdic bail-out effort. The impact of insuring agency assistance measures, together with periodicity of audit and other kind of intervention in bank troubles, detract from the reliability of the absolute magnitude of insurance premiums. Thus Ronn and Verma model the effect of Fdic's policies – namely direct assistance and purchase and assumption options – by assuming that Fdic allows banks to operate with a negative net worth up to a certain point ρ expressed as a percentage of the total bank debt B. Therefore if the value of the bank happens to fall between ρB and B the insuring agency infuses up to $(1 - \rho)B$ to make the value equal to B, while should the value fall below ρB, it steps into dissolve the assets of the bank. Essentially the two authors introduced a policy parameter, ρ, in the option pricing model, which is assumed as fixed, known and cross sectionally constant.

Put option model for deposit insurance premium has been ulteriorly extended by McCulloch (1985), by taking into account the volatility of interest rates which is considered as an important variable affecting the value of the insurance.

McCulloch' model differs from those mentioned above principally in that it assumes a stable process instead of a diffusion process for bank assets and liabilities. The net worth is not a continuous function of time as it is assumed by the original option pricing model; the net worth undergoes discontinuities such as those which occur under a Paretian stable process in continuous time.[4]

According to McCulloch, the Black-Scoles option pricing formula used by Merton and others to evaluate deposit insurance arbitrarily assumes a normal distribution of bank failure and therefore greatly understates the value of deposit insurance if in fact the distribution is non Gaussian. Thus the assumption of a Paretian distribution for the event of bank failure makes the model more general.[5]

In terms of bank net worth the stable distribution assumption means that it could pass from positive to negative in one instant, giving the insuring agency no time to act. Thus McCulloch determines the value per year insurance with continuous surveillance, computed as a fraction of liabilities in the expression:[6]

$$I = \lambda H(r,\alpha) / r \qquad (9)$$

where

λ	=	annual rate of discontinuities in the value of bank's assets large enough to cause insolvency;
$H(r,\alpha)=$		expected cost of failure if a failure occurs;
r	=	$1 - q$ = bank ratio of liabilities to assets.

Estimates of deposit insurance value based on this modified framework show an extreme variability, this variability depending on the volatility of interest rates. Therefore, an efficient insurance pricing scheme must consider the predictability of interest rates.

4.1.2 The cases against pricing insurance

While risk-sensitive premium is one of the most traditional remedies proposed for dealing with banks that take excessive risk because of deposit insurance, it is the most opposed by many critics. Although there is a widespread support for this proposal that goes over the theoretical development mentioned above, many showed practical implementing issues together with probable distorsive effects in the financial industry.

Probably most of these critics run into the "ideal" system that risk-related insurance premiums takes upon itself, appealing to a more realistic view for the solution of current deposit insurance problems. Even if desiderable, they believe that a goal of variable premiums is impossible to achieve.

Thus one significant aspect of deposit insurance pricing is the identification and the measurement of θ_i in equation (1), that is the vector of risk characteristic of the ith bank. As long as θ_i could be priced no perverse incentive problems would exist in protecting deposits. Each bank would be correctly sorted into its own risk class by premiums set according to the ex-ante risk characteristics of that bank, and similarly the incentive problem would not exist since premiums would instantaneously adjust to reflect the risk of the bank's current and future operation.

The actual implementation of such a pricing scheme requires a considerable degree of information, perfection and continuous surveillance and auditing by regulators. Precise risk-return schedules have to be known in advance for all existing on and off balance sheet activities and, at the some time, this knowledge has to regard all other potential activities. Then, for the useful identification of θ_i feasible measurements of risk and a complete information on bank activities as a base for assessing premiums, is required. Clearly the assumption of a full information world is very restrictive and unrealistic and it would make the same existence of banks unnecessary.

Let us consider more deeply these issues concerning pricing deposit insurance scheme implementation. The fair measurement of bank's risk is crucial to implement an effective pricing premium for deposit insurance. In fact any component of overall risks that were underpriced might still attract overinvestment by some banks, while any components of risks that were overpriced would too severely discourage productive investment. The greater the likelihood of risk mismeasurement, the less attractive variable premium insurance becomes.

The identification of factors affecting the choice of a proxy for risk is not self-evident. Many different variables have been tried with varying degrees of success. The Fdic (1983) has suggested some key variables: credit risks, as potential losses from defaults on debt obligations; interest rate risk, as potential deterioration of interest margins from adverse interest rate movements; liquidity risk, as potential loss from untimely asset liquidation or abnormally-high interest costs incurred to meet funding requirements and finally moral hazard risk. Nevertheless any listing of risk component for banks is not exhaustive. The presence of off-balance-sheet items and unforseen source of risk, that have continued to emerge in banking intermediation activities, as well as the potential bank's propension to fraud make any attempt to construct θ_i an unsuccessful and useless effort. Empirical estimates provided by Marcus and Shaked, McCulloch and Pennacchi (1983) have based the measurement of risk of bank assets – as we have seen – through an analysis of return on bank stocks. The basic idea was that in an efficient capital market, investors' benefits regarding the riskiness of the bank are reflected instantaneously in bank stock prices. However, this measurement of bank risk lies on the existing relationship between the variance of stock returns and the variance of returns on underlying assets, whose identification is quite complex, so that the total assets return volatility measures may be mispecified. Moreover assets return volatility is usually imputed using historical stock return data. As many showed, implicit market forecast of future return volatility takes into account factors other then historical return data.

A contribution to the understanding risk measurement difficulties has been provided by Herring and Vankudre (1987). They showed that growth opportunities which cannot be converted to cash under condition of financial distress, are critical determinants of a bank's choice of risk and therefore of an insuring agency's forecasting of bank riskiness. Along Herring and Vankudre reasoning G_z, which reflects the bank's economic rents or quasirents, it is part of bank's economic net worth not convertible into cash and can cause banks with identical net worth to have very different preference risk. In particular banks for which G_z is a negligible proportion of total assets are much more likely to engage in go-for-broke behaviour than banks for which G_z is a substantial proportion of total assets. So that it is likely to be counterproductive to charge a risk-rated insurance premium irrespective of G_z, to a low G_z bank. That bank will increase its preferred level of risk. In this case an attempt to constraint a particular kind of risk-taking may actually have the perverse effects of inducing the bank to choose a new kind of risk-taking, since the device was not fairly adjusted. In terms of θ_i, a determinant component, G_z, has been disregarded and probably it would not have been otherwise since G_z is intrinsically difficult to evaluate.

A practical suggestion for a risk-related insurance scheme has been proposed by Fdic (1983) with the objective to overcome the requirement of sophisticated risk quantification technologies without renouncing to efficiency improvement associated to a pricing system. The Fdic proposed system assumes that banks can be sorted yearly into discrete risk classes, namely three of them: normal, high and very high. The bank sorting is based on credit risk and interest-rate risk as they relate to capital. So that, according to the proposal, banks assigned to very high class are those operating with dangerously low capital ratios or those viewed as having both high credit risk and high interest-rate risk; banks assigned to the high risk class are those having either high interest risk or

120

high credit risk; all other banks are in the normal class and they are supposed to be the vast majority.

The valuation criteria envisaged by Fdic for banks' risk selection are founded on extremely observable risk characteristics. A part from the restricted interpretation of θ_i vector components, since only the bank knows its true risk of failure the θ_i indicators suggested by Fdic program are likely to be imperfect measurements of risk unless incentives exist to signal the true nature of risk.[7] Furthermore the true loss distribution for a bank is unobservable ex-ante and can only be discovered ex-post.

The system proposed by Fdic denounces the punishing effects of a pricing insurance scheme based on after the fact observations, rather than points out its effectiveness on modifying banks perverse behaviour before the fact. A modification of the current deposit insurance arrangement toward pricing premium aims to reinstate insurance's statuted purpose of preventing failures. The practical effects of a risk-adjusted premium that operates in Fdic advanced fashion would be to penalize losses after they have been incurred rather than to discourage the behaviour which leads to the losses beforehand.

As Horvitz (1983) argued, the true problem with risk-related premiums is the difficulty of measuring risks ex-ante. If the riskiness of certain activities or assets is recognized by the premium system only after they have resulted in loss, then the premium structure does not serve its purposes of inhibiting risk-taking. Furthermore it could be harmful by making worse institutions already in trouble: a higher premium on top of higher capital requirements may finish them off.

Thus, a pricing reformed premium structure based on the available risk measurement techniques, might alter bank behaviour in possibly unpredictable or perverse ways. It is possible that such a system could result in a greater distortion of the allocation of resources than the present flat-premium system.

These perverse effects of risk-sensitive premium have been carefully studied by Chan and Mak (1985) employing a welfare analysis. The aim of their work was to answer whether a risk-sensitive premium necessarily leads to an optimal level of bank risk-taking and therefore whether it necessarily improves the welfare of depositors. The model they develop to answer this question is a three operators classes model, depositors, banks and Fdic, where a complex regulation policy affects the banking industry.

Depositors are small savers with limited investment alternatives, they are risk-adverse and will only invest in risk-free assets. The Fdic is assumed to be the guarantor of their welfare and takes on the responsibilities of providing them deposit insurance which ensures a sure return. Then Fdic's objective is to maximize depositors' welfare, that is to maximize the rate r, subject to some conditions, the most important of which is that the probability of bank failures does not exceed an acceptable level $\hat{\pi}$. Finally banks compete for deposits and invest the proceeds and their own capital in assets. They are assumed to choose assets so as to maximize their expected profit subject to the regulated banking environment. In this environment it is possible to illustrate the effect of a risk-sensitive schedule.

Suppose the Fdic's optimal policy is:

$$(r°, p°, e°, y°)$$

where $r°$ = a level of deposit rate ceiling;
          $p°$ = insurance premium;
          $e°$ = minimal bank capital;
          $y°$ = expected return on assets.

Let us suppose now the Fdic still sets rate ceiling $r°$ but lets the banks freely choose their investment y for which they will be charged the risk-sensitive premium $p^*(y)$ and have to put up the capital $e^*(y)$.[8] If the risk-sensitive premium were efficient in risk management, banks would choose the optimal portfolio $y = y°$. On the contrary the model generates $y \neq y°$. That is the risk-sensitive premium and capital schedule $p^*(\cdot), e^*(\cdot)\}$ will encourage the banks to take higher risk asset $(y > y°)$ increasing their payoff and that of the Fdic at the expense of the small savers and increasing the likelihood of bank insolvency. Corresponding to the higher risk asset y the probability of bank insolvency, in fact, will exceed the acceptable level $\hat{\pi}$.

The upshot of Chan-Mak's work is that risk-related premiums may not improve the efficiency in managing the risk-taking of banks and, therefore in risk management of the insurance system.

A relevant last issue concerns pricing deposit insurance. Considering deposit insurance effects on resources allocation and on financial system stability, its relationship with other existing protection devices takes relevance. If a risk-related premium were implemented assuming its feasibility, which could be deposit insurance and Llr interactions?

Kanatas (1986) explored this question by formalizing the joint pricing of deposit insurance and discount window advances with the assumption of private information. The theoretical framework implemented by Kanatas has generated a quite obvious conclusion: any policy that prices the banks' deposit insurance but maintains the current discount window arrangements will prompt banks to substitute uninsured deposits[9] for insured ones and thereby escapes the discipline of both the market and the insurance pricing policy. This happens because the provision of emergency funds through the discount window is an implicit guarantee of uninsured deposits to the extent that banks experiencing withdrawals are provided funds. Let us consider that risk-sensitive deposit insurance pricing is adopted and this pricing mechanism is not extended to the credit eventually provided by the discount window. The lender of last resort in emergency lends at the market rate whereas private lenders refuse to lend at any finite price, so that banks will have an incentive to substitute uninsured deposits for insured ones, saving insurance premiums.

This last consideration raises a substantial issue on pricing deposit insurance implementation. Together with risk measurement problems, which practically prevent insurance premiums from being fairly adjusted to bank riskiness, and with the actual difficulty to consider every bank's assets component in constructing the base for assessing premiums, an issue of general effectiveness of the safety net for the financial system takes relevance. Risk-adjusted premiums may have perverse effects on banks' behaviour towards risk-taking. Furthermore they characterize an insurance schedule that may be incompatible with the objective the regulator pursues through other protecting instruments. These arguments throw a different light on the current deposit insurance system founded on a risk-irrespective flat premium.

4.1.3 Macroeconomic issues on risk-adjusted deposit insurance

Risk-based deposit insurance premium proposals aim to improve deposit insurance efficiency thereby introducing price mechanism into the current system. If the insurance premium is set correctly it would induce the optimal degree of risk-taking, reducing banks' behaviour towards moral hazard. In fact a variable-rate deposit insurance scheme would impose a marginal penalty associated with additional risk-taking. The trade-off between two potential sources of financial instability, bank runs and bank risk-taking, would finally disappear.

The ideal system suggested by the supporters of risk-sensitive premiums is found on an actuarial optimality. The premium is "fair" to the extent that it is actuarially-based. However this does not assure that the premium is consequently fair and optimal from a social point of view. Macroeconomic issues are also relevant in dealing with optimality of a financial regulatory policy .

Social effects of a variable-rate insurance have been analysed by Goodman and Santomero (1986) in a seminal enlightened paper. Along the Goodman Santomero work a model of financial and non-financial firm is outlined to show that a move from a fixed rate deposit insurance regime to a risk-based variable-rate regime will constrain bank risk-taking. This will lower the social cost of financial sector bankruptcy, while raising the costs of real-sector bankruptcy: the financial effect may be not costless.

Let us assume there is only one source of risk for banks, credit risk, so that the total variability of banks' earnings stems from credit risk. The ith bank has the following balance sheet:

$$L_i + S_i = D_i + C_i$$

where
L_i = risky loans;
S_i = risk-free loans and securities;
D_i = deposits;
C_i = capital.

L_i, S_i, D_i, C_i are positive for all banks. The bank is assumed to have some monopoly power in the deposit market.

Deposit insurance is currently fixed such that the rate is the same regardless of asset composition and it is captured by the model by assuming that premiums are imposed at any equal rate loans and securities, that is

$$\alpha_1 = \alpha_2 = k$$

124

where α_1 = insurance rate on loans;

           α_2 = insurance rate on securities;

           k = constant.

The model, where capital C_i is fixed, considers deposit insurance on the asset side of the balance sheet, rather than on the deposit side. Differently from this fixed rate scheme, a variable-rate scheme imposes a higher rate on loans than on securities, that is $\alpha_1 > \alpha_2$.

From an initial point of identical premiums let us suppose now that $d\alpha_1 > 0$ and $d\alpha_2 < 0$. Intuitively as the insurance of loans gets more expensive, the i_{th} bank will make fewer loans and as insurance on securities gets less expensive, the i_{th} bank will make fewer loans and will issue more securities and deposits. Aggregating over all banks, a change in the cost structure of deposit insurance from fixed-rate to variable-rate will result in a contraction in the loan supply curve. Since the loans demand curve has a constant downward slope, this will result in an higher interest rate (r_L) and a lower volume for marketed loans.

On the corporate firm side, the value of the firm – a single input and a single output firm – if it is solvent is given by

$$v = Pf(L) - (1 + r_L)L + A$$

where L = total cost of labour;

           $f(L)$ = quantity of output produced;

           P = selling price of output;

           v_L = landing rate;

           L = loan quantity;

           A = assets.

This corporate model assumes fixed assets A, which are borrowed from the bank at a rate r_L at the beginning of the period to pay labour. If the firm is unable to repay the principal and interest on its bank loans it is bankrupt. In this case the firm must liquidate its assets at a value A', which is the market's perception of firm assets alternative use.

Since a shifting from fixed-rate to a variable rate insurance causes an increase in the equilibrium lending rate – as argued above – firms will face an increase cost for their assets. This will make the chance of corporate insolvency higher and hence the probability (θ) that shareholders will lose the value ($A - A'$).

Let us analyse the expected change in social costs of a change in the insurance rate, taking account of financial and real sector issues. If α_1 and α_2 are set so that a rate-variable insurance is established, the marginal social cost of financial sector bankruptcy is given by

$$\sum_{i-1}^{N} \lambda' \partial G_i = \Delta ES_f < 0$$

where N is the number of financial institutions; ∂G_i is the variation in insurer's liabilities decline associated with i_{th} bank's adjustment to the shift in insurance pricing. is the monotonic function relating insurer losses to the social cost of bank failure. Finally ES_i is the expected social cost of bankruptcy in the financial sector.

The social cost of bankruptcy for the real sector can be derived in a analogous manner, taking into account that the cost of real sector bankruptcy is the divergence between the value of the present owners A, relative to its next-use of A'. So that given a fixed probability of the jth firm insolvency (θ) the expected social cost of bankruptcy at the corporate level is

$$ES_{rj} = \theta_j(A - A')$$

The marginal social cost if insurance rates α_1 and α_2 are changed, is:

$$\sum_{i-1}^{M} \partial ES_{rj} = \Delta ES_r > 0$$

where M is the number of firms and ∂ES_{rj} is the effect of the alteration in the deposit insurance pricing system on the cost of the jth firm bankruptcy.[10]

ΔES_f and ΔES_r allow us to focus on the total social cost of a financial regulatory policy such as variable-premium insurance deposits. In fact the effects in the economic system of such a policy is quantified by:

$$\Delta ES_f + \Delta ES_r = \Delta ES$$

The optimal deposit insurance is one in which α_1 and α_2 are set so that

$$\Delta ES = 0$$

that is

$$\Delta ES_r = \Delta ES_f$$

To achieve this goal, however, the insurance should be underpriced, that is the optimal insurance premium structure from a societal point of view is not actuarially sound. This arises because if the ratio of α_1 and α_2 is set so that ΔES_f is identically zero in the neighbourhood of the optimum, however ΔES_r is unambiguously positive throughout the relevant range since

$$\partial ES_{rj} = \frac{\partial \theta_j}{\partial r_L}(A_j - A'_j) + \theta_j \frac{\partial A'_j}{\partial r_L} \frac{dr_L}{d\alpha_1} \delta\alpha_1 > 0$$

both terms are unambiguously non-negative.

Therefore it must be the case that the differential premium for risky loans at the micro optimum is too high. Lowering the premium differential to achieve the societal optimum implies that the resultant premium schedule will underprice risky loans and must be actuarially unsound.

This conclusion implies that the financial policy goal of social cost minimization is not pursued through an actuarially fair insurance pricing and then both microeconomic and macroeconomic optimal objectives have to be taken in account to evaluate the effectiveness of political intervention in the financial sector. It is not necessarily undesirable to price deposit insurance on a variable-pricing scheme. However, there must be an explicit recognition that it shifts risk from the financial sector to the real sector.

The pricing deposit insurance proposal, which is based only on microeconomic consideration, shows its weakness as other piecemeal schemes to improve resources allocation.

A fundamental problem with pricing deposit insurance is created by the fact that since resource allocation is not perfect in all other sections of the economy, it does not necessarily follow that setting prices of risk taking for the financial intermediaries equal to the marginal cost would improve resource allocation.

These issues stand out the current flat premium insurance scheme as a reasonable second-best solution.

A fixed-rate deposit insurance provides a risk transfer from the uninsured real sector to the insured financial sector since financial institutions take more risk while real-sector agents assume less risk. In this sense fixed-rate deposit insurance plays a crucial macroeconomic stabilization role.[11]

In terms of Goodman-Santomero's theoretical framework this deposit insurance stabilization role can be clearly showed by considering a dynamic world. Economic activity, Y, is assumed to follow a traditional business cycle. Variation in Y causes variation in θ_j, that is bankruptcy probability, and in bankruptcy cost $(A - A')$. If the business cycle is high in relation to its mean value and a risk-based premium insurance regime is in place, standard measures of risk would typically indicate a lower level of credit risk and would exaggerate the easing of credit. On the contrary, during a cycle downturn, raising the insurance premiums would discourage lending, exactly when the economy needed easier credit.

A flat-rate deposit insurance system, while creates a moral hazard and prevents depositors from exerting discipline on banks, serves as useful macroeconomic stabilization tool.

4.2 MARKET DISCIPLINE SOLUTIONS

Risk-related pricing of deposit insurance suggests a way to deal with insurance deposit incentives to increase banks' moral hazard which is based in a certain manner on regulation. Banks' risk changes have to be maintained and measured by authorities making rule and supervision.

A different way to face the moral hazard issue calls for greater reliance on market discipline. The presence of market-determined incentives could serve the soundness of a deposit insurance system by stimulating depository institutions to control risk by their own. In contrast to regulation, market discipline seeks to make it in the economic interest of bankers to act in ways consistent with the preservation of deposit insurance funds by making market participants bear more of the costs resulting from risky activities. Therefore market policy options aim to carry out a co-insurance built-in system.

4.2.1 Sized based deposit insurance

As long as all depositors are insured, explicitly or implicitly, market discipline arising from depositor incentives to monitor the portfolio behaviour of banks, is neutralized. A depositor who is somewhat at risk is likely to be induced to evaluate the risk level of his bank, to compare it with that of competing institutions and either replace his money in a sounder bank or else demand a higher interest rate at the riskier bank. The co-insurance inherent to a partial deposit insurance thus enhances depositor banks' monitoring. This effect would serve to increase the penalty associated with undertaking additional risk so that bank shareholders would act in a more prudent way.

Deposit insurance, like a financial policy device, is not designed to protect a bank against failure, rather it is aimed to promote financial stability by preventing bank runs from occurring. Nevertheless the pervasive use of merger or direct bailout in the event of bank failure rescues all depositors and bankers from bearing any costs in an insolvency, so that depositors have little reason to pay close attention to the condition of their banks.

For this reason it is argued that the provision of uninsured depositors, or depositors partially insured, in the measure of a percentage of their deposits or the provision of depositors which receive only partial compensation in the event of failure equal to the estimated market value of the bank assets, would make some depositors pledging themselves for market discipline. Co-insurance provided by uninsured or by partially insured depositors would re-build market discipline effects on banks' risk-taking behaviour.

In theory, the U.S. deposit insurance system provides a co-insurance mechanism. A statutory limit on deposit insurance is set up to $100,000. As a bank becomes insolvent, Fdic should let it fail buying off its insured depositors, those up to $100,000 and, as receivers, liquidating its assets for the benefit of other creditors. In practice, a 100 per cent de facto coverage has been provided by virtue of the actual Fdic failure resolution policies.

The adoption of the so called "too big to fail" doctrine, in fact, induced Fdic to opt different arrangements: merging the failed bank into a sound one; taking over and temporarily managing a failing institution with a view to restructuring it and selling it in the future; selling a failed

129

institution's insured deposits only, so that uninsured depositors receive an immediate credit for the amount of their claims that the Fdic estimates will untimely be recovered (modified pay-off solution); the purchase and assumption resolution. Especially this last arrangement, very popular among Fdic interventions, has made de facto coverage for depositors, at least in large size institutions, unlimited.

Also the British deposit insurance system is based on depositors' co-insurance. The coverage of the insurance extends up to the 75 per cent of deposits under £ 10,000, so that only small depositors are protected but however their incentives to monitor bank risk-taking are not completely undone by insurance.

Considering the market discipline incentives inherent to a deposit insurance system where depositors co-insure their claims on bank, many have supported it with theoretical and empirical arguments. Baer and Brawer (1986) have given empirical evidence to the statement that uninsured depositors are a crucial source of market discipline. In particular, they tested the hypothesis that certificates of deposit markets charge U.S. riskier banks higher rates, that is, CDs are risk-sensitive and act controlling bank risk behaviour. Their estimates result over a period running from 1979/4 to 1982/3, suggest in fact that CD holders demand higher rates when banks' market to asset ratio is low or when volatility of bank stock returns is high. Uninsured CDs holders therefore set risk premiums as if they are at least partially at risk. This leads to the imposition of market discipline in a non disruptive fashion, on large institutions that are most dependent on the money market for funding.

Comparing the pricing mechanism of a variable-rate deposit insurance with the pricing mechanism associated with a size based deposit insurance, the latter acts through deposit risk premiums and funds supply. Instead of facing a rising schedule of insurance premiums as it takes more risk, a bank would face a rising schedule of interest rates with a similar impact on bank earnings and capital. Nevertheless, the co-insurance system lets the "price" of risk to be set by market agents with demand and supply adjustments, according with different perceptions of bank riskiness, whereas variable premium insurance sets the price of risk ex-ante according with a standard perception of bank riskiness.

Some problems with this market discipline approach to deposit insurance moral hazard issue raise. The most important regards its underestimation of bank run costs, including contagion effects by large risk-adverse depositors. Some depositors might simply withdraw their funds rather than accept a higher interest rate as compensation for higher risk. This is likely to occur especially when a borrowing rate grows so high as to be unsustainable compared to lending rates. Furthermore the lack of upside variability in interest rate makes it rational to withdraw rather than to accept downside risk.

Therefore a severe policy of partial insurance can have destabilizing consequences.[12] While uninsured depositors may well look more closely than they do in a de facto 100 per cent deposit coverage at the credit worthiness of a bank before placing their funds, their reactions to higher perceived levels of risk are probably to be compromising for the stability of the financial system. Moreover, since most uninsured depositors have short term deposits, they are capable of withdrawing quickly at the first rumor of specific trouble, regardless of the fact that the whole market shows enlarging and distorting signals for runs.

The price mechanism does not take into account the global cost of a run, by reflecting anything but the private cost of bank failure. Furthermore a quite straightforword expedient to avoid the size limit of deposit insurance coverage and to carry out a de facto 100 per cent protection does exist. In fact, although the coverage is usually applied on customer per bank basis, coverage can be extended by holding a number of accounts under different names in a single institution. Large deposits may also gain additional protection by virtue of the fact that in the event of a failure, they will only be asked to repay an amount equal to their net indebtedness to that institution; that is their total deposits may be offset against loans even if they exceed the insurance limit. Thus a deposit brokerage system rises from the provision of co-insurance allowing for a nearly limitless extention of de jure protection beyond the virtual "ceiling" posed by the insurance scheme.

A finally problematical issue with a depositors' co-insurance system concerns the likely increasing role of the discount window. In fact, some risk-shifting is likely to be place from uninsured depositors to the lender of last resort. If Llr is willing to make discount loans to meet all bank liquidity troubles, it is quite probable that banks will use these funds to substitute for those withdrawals by large risk-adverse depositors.[13] This might, cause discount window to assist banks without a predictable limit.

Thus the main argument against partial payoff arrangement for deposit insurance is that market discipline it provided appears to require even more stringent control over the supply and pricing,of borrowed reserves than has otherwise been needed. Banks coming to Llr for liquidity crises have to be regulated severely. The market discipline associated with the co-insurance system would have, hence, high costs and on the other hand it would not necessarily relax the need for regulation constraints on bank's behaviour towards risk.

4.2.2 Maturity based partial deposit insurance

A different manner of imposing market discipline via a partial deposit insurance system focuses on deposit maturity rather than size. According to this proposal, suggested by Furlong (1984) among others, all deposits which are liquid would be insured while those that are relatively illiquid would be at risk. Thereby uninsured depositors would have no incentive to withdraw at the first rumor of specific trouble. They would do that only at penalty cost so that they would have incentive similar to those of bank bond holders in monitoring bank performance.

The maturity-based deposit insurance rationale is funded on the idea that short-term deposits, particularly transaction deposits which are made available on demand, are the primary source of bank runs while longer-term become a source of run subsequently if depositors decline to roll over this type of bank debt.

Restricting bank coverage to liquid deposits, regardless of size is clearly consistent with the deposit insurance goal of avoiding the costs of bank run without inducing banks to undertake excessive risk. Compared with sized-based partial insurance, the system suggested by Furlong has clearer ground. Furlong argues that imposing a greater risk on large depositors is consistent only with the "small-depositor" protection rationale for deposit insurance. Increasing the riskiness of all large-denomination deposits, on the other hand, is not compatible with the objective of achieving stability in the banking system, which provides a better reason for having deposit insurance. Thus to prevent runs on banks being the first role for insuring deposits and since the mismatch of asset and liability durations contributes to the vulnerability of the banking system, a co-insurance provision on the basis of account maturity might be effective in enhancing depositors' discipline on bank behaviour. In essence Furlong states that while the threat posed by instantly callable deposits is well-established, connection between the size of deposit accounts and the probability of bank runs does not appear so evident.

As with size-based deposit insurance, some problems arise with implementing a maturity-based scheme. The first issue arises in selecting the appropriate definition of a short maturity deposit; in particular this problems regards where the maturity spectrum should be split to select liquid and illiquid deposits. As Furlong pointed out, the longest maturity eligible for insurance coverage should allow sufficient time for determining the financial condition of bank examination. Furthermore the degree of "runnability" of different maturity is not immediate and it is not necessarily uniform across deposits of the same maturity given the different covenants in deposit contracts.

Maturity selection of deposits also depends upon the penalty costs of payments and upon other disincentives to cash in early which are the disincentives for uninsured depositors to withdraw and then to trigger bank runs.

A second problem with maturity-based coverage is that over time some maturity switching might occur, changing the maturity structure of bank deposits. As some uninsured depositors move to short-term accounts, that is to deposits just below the insurance maturity ceiling, the average maturity of deposits will be reduced.

Regarding to this scheme Carns (1989) pointed out some macroeconomic consequences of great concern. The maturity-based insurance provides an effective subsidy to short-term accounts. In so doing it also provides a sort of intervention in the financial market which could distort that market discipline enhancing what it is aimed to pursue.

4.2.3 Closure rule

Deposit insurance is not intended to end all bank failures. Its ideal goal is to facilitate the quick and orderly resolution of bank failures so as to limit their effects on the financial system. Any change in the current insurance systems which is oriented to improve market discipline is therefore oriented to make failures less likely by making them a real possibility. If creditors face a real possibility of loss, they might be more inclined to keep a close control on what bank managers are doing.

Most current deposit insurance systems let an institution operate until its regulatory capital has been exhausted so economic net worth has long since gone negative. This closure rule allows banks to act during a period where they are insolvent that it is likely they are taking in less income than they are paying out as interest expense. Furthermore the managers of troubled institutions have incentives to gamble making extremely risky loans in the hopes that the funded projects will succeed and thereby generate high returns. High risk assets also carry a high probability of losses so that depositors together with insurance funds are at risk. Finally the eventual uninsured depositors have time to withdraw their funds, making bank balance weaker.

As Horvitz (1983) stressed, the losses of the deposit insurance systems are not closely related to the risk of insured institutions, rather they are more a function of the timing of the closing of a failed bank.

Thus the negative outcome of policy decisions to allow insolvent institutions to continue operating could be reduced, if not eliminated, by a timely reorganization/closure intervention. The establishment of these alternative policies that facilitate the closure of insured banks before the economic value of their net worth becomes negative would introduce market discipline in handling bank failures, in so doing they would prevent bank insolvencies from inflicting severe losses on the deposit insurance funds and on society.

Benston (1988) has supported the proposal for the insurance structure reform relying on a more effective market discipline. Benston's arguments pro the enforcement of a timely closure rule are fundamentally three. The first points out that the effective elimination of losses from bank failure would reduce the need for insurance premiums in excess of those necessary to meet the operational expenses of the insurance, including upgraded and more frequent monitoring of insured institutions and the development of accurate market value accounting systems. The second benefit of instituting a timely reorganization policy is that the risk characteristics of banks would be unimportant. To the extent that banks are capable of acting with their own equity funds, there would be little justification for imposing regulatory constraints on the nature of the activities in which banks may or may not be engaged solely on consideration of risk.

The last argument focuses on the important competitive implications of the current insurance policies which threaten failed banks unequally according to their size. Uninsured depositors at large banks are reimbursed in full in the event of bank failure, regardless of the bank's condition, while uninsured depositors at small banks frequently suffer losses related to the market value of bank's assets. The partiality of the "too-large-to fail" principle would be eliminated by the implementation of e timely failure resolution rule. In fact, it is aimed at preventing depositor losses by closing banks regardless of their size, location, and the nature of their business.

Thus timely reorganization or closure may be more efficient than reduction in insurance coverage, co-insurance or risk-sensitive premiums: it guarantees a low premium cost to banks, a great freedom from regulation of bank risks and activities and equity in treating banks in similar financial predicaments.

In spite of its attractiveness, prompt closing is neither easy nor costless. It is not easy because of the difficulties which relate the implementation of market value accounting and more frequent monitoring and because of the difficulties of applying stringent standard insolvency similar to that for non-banking firms to banks. Furthermore prompt closing is not costless because it imposes costs on the community.

Nevertheless, since deposit insurance must serve the goal of protecting the financial system from instability, via depositor protection, and it must act as a loss controlling instrument it has to be structured so as to allow banks to fail limiting depositors losses and not to prevent banks from failing. Furthermore, any kind of switch in current insurance scheme, aimed to improve depositor-discipline, would not be able to yield its potential benefits unless failure resolution methods also were altered.

4.3 INCREASED DISCLOSURE

Market efficiency can also be enhanced by information disclosure. In the case of the banking industry, public disclosure of information is usually controlled by regulatory policy to prevent confidence problems and runs on banks.

Thus pervasive asymmetries of information are implemented by regulators as a device against financial instability. However it can be argued that constraints on public information may increase the probability of widespread runs or panics based on rumours.

135

It is difficult, in fact, for investors to distinguish good banks from bad since there are no incentives for bad banks to signal their true failure risk. A more disclose information, by showing banks' real financial and operating position might allow depositors to make more adequate judgement and then impose market discipline in the appropriate manner.

Information concerning the true financial conditions of banks could be greatly improved if banks were required to report estimates of the market values of their assets and liabilities. In fact market values give the most accurate representation of a bank's net worth. Under the current accounting standards, based on book value of balance items, changes in financial variables might drive the market value of a bank's assets below that of its liabilities, without being made evident by accounts until loan loss reserves were increased, part of the asset written off or the asset sold.

Deposit insurance would benefit from market value accounting in that it reduces the potential loss of their funds. In fact depositors, uninsured depositors, would impose their discipline on banks' behaviour and regulators could be capable of closing a bank when its market value first goes negative rather than waiting for the book value to go negative. The regulatory policy on banks would be more effective in controlling banks' operations and in monitoring their outcome. Furthermore considering bank behaviour, making assets to market would reduce some perverse incentives existing under the present system to sell high quality assets to realize gains while retaining poor quality assets to avoid recognizing losses.

Despite these advantages of banking policy, as well as of deposit insurance effectiveness improvement, the feasibility of market value accounting is questionable. The main problem concerns the valuing of loans for which no secondary markets exist. For example loans to consumer or medium and small sized businesses are difficult to value since their quality is difficult to quantify.

Furthermore, even if market value accounting were established as a device to increase disclosure about banks' true net worth information, it would tend not to increase discipline by depositors unless combined with explicit partial nonpayment of uninsured deposits. If all depositors were fully protected they would have little incentive to collect and to react to any information regarding the financial prospects of their banks.

Finally, a punitive effect on banks caused by increased disclosure has been argued by some. In fact, once a bank has faced troubles public reaction could make it harder for that bank to recover from the crisis, making failure more likely.

4.4 RISK-BASED CAPITAL

Deposit insurance limits market incentives to control bank behaviour towards risk-taking without substituting regulatory constraints in their place through a variable rate pricing regime. A well-developed system of bank supervision, as distinct from regulation, provides a complementary form of constraint by supervising bank performances so that if bank examinations were very frequent – at limit continuous – and the compliance with the closure rule occurred as soon as a bank is perceived to be in trouble, the costs associated with bank failure would be minimized, both costs to the insurer and depositors and to the society.

Since bank examination cannot take place on a continuous basis, the crucial variable for a preventive monitoring is the banks' capital ratio. This suggests that strictly enforced minimum capital standard or capital ratio to overall bank risk, may be imposed to control bank activities and hence their riskiness.

A number of authors have suggested that any reforms in deposit insurance pricing or insurance coverage should be supplemented by adjustments to bank primary capital adequacy ratios. Others have viewed bank capital as self-insurance or co-insurance of banks with the insurer, so that it is rational for the insurer to limit its exposure by demanding increased capital ratios: such a solution makes banks aware of the costs they impose on deposit insurance funds.

Capital standards' supporters look at stockholders for the application of market discipline to banks. Since they absorb losses first a sufficiently high equity investment would inhibit them strongly from taking risks.

The capital adequacy of depository institutions whereas deposits are insured by a third party has been investigated by Sharpe (1978). Assuming a case where the insurer charges a fixed premium per unit on all deposits, Sharpe considers the capital adequacy issue in terms of present value of the insurer's liability. That is, the insured depository institutions have an adequate amount of capital to the extent that the predetermined fixed premium is sufficient to avoid liabilities for the insurer greater than its reserves, or conversely, to prevent insurer net worth from becoming negative. In other words, the insurer should require ex-ante that

$$\frac{D_{Ft} - D_t}{D_{Ft}} \leq \rho \tag{10}$$

where ρ is the fixed per-unit premium; D_t is the value of the deposit claims and D_{Ft} is the amount the deposit claims would be worth at time t if they were default-free.[14]

If condition (10) is met, capital is adequate, in fact $(D_{Ft} - D_t)$ is the present value of insurer's liability, and ρD_{Ft} is the insurance premium so that must be

$$D_{Ft} - D_t \leq \rho D_{Ft} \tag{11}$$

The required condition (10), since ρ is predetermined, depends on the ratio on the left, which, on the basis of a complete market state-preference approach, Sharpe identifies as a function of bank capital coverage and its riskiness.

Figure 4.1 represent the relationship between the ratio $(D_{Ft} - D_t)/D_{Ft}$ and A_t/D_{Ft} at time $t = 0$. Simple monotonic transformations on the horizontal axis can describe capital-deposit and capital-asset ratios. Given the relevant risk r_s^a and r_s^e, where the former is the return on bank's assets from time $t = 0$ to time 1 when state s of the world at time 1 obtains, and the latter is the "default-free" return on the bank's deposit in state s, then an increase in the ratio of assets to the default free value of deposits will reduce the per-unit value of the insurer liability at a decreasing rate. For any amount of risk, there is some amount of capital that makes the per-unit liability equal to any preselected premium. For example if the given per-unit premium were ρ^*, the appropriate amount of capital would be that which provides an asset-to-default deposit ratio of $(A_0/D_{F0})^*$. Further given the relevant risks, the present value of the insurer's liability can be reduced by increasing the value of assets by an infusion of new capital.

On the other hand Sharpe points out that the present value of the insurer's liability depends also on the risk of the bank's assets, the interest rate risk associated with deposits and on the relationship between the two.

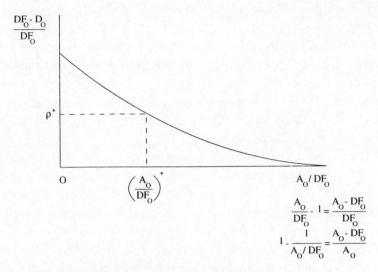

$$\frac{A_O}{DF_O} - 1 = \frac{A_O - DF_O}{DF_O}$$

$$1 - \frac{1}{A_O/DF_O} = \frac{A_O - DF_O}{A_O}$$

Figure 4.1: The relationship between asset to default-free
value of deposit ratio and insurer' liability at time t=O

In conclusion the actual capacity of the insurer to act according to its aim to make the system safe by covering depositors' claims, depends on its capacity to bring in enough resources, and this again depends on the capital adequacy of insured depository institutions. Thus Sharpe's analysis makes it clearer that banks capital requirements are crucial in determining deposit insurance system effectiveness.

Also Kim and Santomero (1988) have stressed the crucial role of capital regulation in the banking industry where a fixed-rate deposit insurance pricing is provided. They pointed out the co-insurance aspect of capital regulation since higher capital levels require the bank to absorb greater losses in the event of failure and encourage additional prudence in management. Nevertheless, they also pointed out that a stringent capital regulation through a simple capital to asset ratio can be an incentive for banks to take more risk by portfolio rearrangements so that the probability of failure may increase for some institutions.

Thus they analyse the theoretical statement of a proposal which suggests a risk-related capital regulation, where the quality of assets and off-balance sheet risk exposure is considered into the calculation of bank's required capital. While Sharpe has conceived bank capital adequacy focusing on deposit insurers' capacity to be solvent, Kim and

Santomero $(K - S)$ look at the behaviour of banks considering also their risk preference structure.

By using a single-period mean-variance model $K - S$ confront the effectiveness of the traditional uniform capital ratio regulation and of the risk-rated capital regulation in controlling the probability of bank insolvency. The latter appears to be potentially more effective to the extent that optimal risk weights chosen and imposed on each bank subject to the regulatory constraint.

Let us consider an optimizing banking firm,[15] under the assumption that capital regulation on its opportunity set is working. The bank's portfolio problem involves the determination of the proportion of each balance sheet item relative to the equity capital. Figure 4.2 describes in a (E, σ) space – where E and σ are respectively the mean over which the bank's strictly quasi-concave objective function U and the standard derivation of return on equity – the global frontier $G_0 \, G_1 \, G_2$ of efficient portfolios. $G_0 \, G_1 \, G_2$ is the Merton hyperbola and is an envelope of efficient frontiers with all levels of equity-to-asset ratio K. As K increases the efficient frontier moves down from $P_0 \, P_1 \, P_2$ to $R_0 \, R_1 \, R_2$, so that as we move up along the global frontier, the underlying portfolio corresponds to a higher expected return on equity E and a lower K, that is a riskier portfolio. In the absence of capital regulation, the global frontier $G_0 \, G_1 \, G_2$ is feasible to a bank.

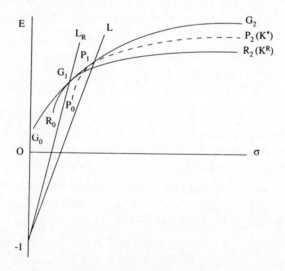

Figure 4.2: The effect of capital regulation
on the probability of insolvency

The figure describes also $R_0 \, G_1 \, R_2$ as the efficient frontier conditional on capital ratio K^R, while $P_0 \, P_1 \, P_2$ is the efficient frontier conditional on capital ratio $K^* < K^R$. Let $P : (E^*, \sigma^*, K^*)$ be the reference portfolio for the discussion of capital regulation,[16] characterized by the relative risk aversion parameter Γ. Bank insolvency is defined as an event where $E \leq -1$, that is the event where the bank's equity capital is completely eliminated in terms of market values. Since the return on equity is normally distributed, the probability of insolvency will satisfy:

$$\text{prob}\,[E \leq -1] = \text{prob} \ \frac{E - E}{\sigma} \leq \frac{-1 - E}{\sigma} = p$$

Thus

$$E = -1 - \phi\,(p)\sigma \quad \text{and} \quad -\phi\,(p)\sigma = \frac{E + 1}{\sigma} \tag{12}$$

where $\phi(\cdot)$ is the inverse of the cumulative standard normal distribution function.

In terms of the graphic, L^R and L allow to compare the risk of different portfolios. In fact equation (12) represents the line connecting $E = -1$ and a chosen portfolio, (E, σ), with a slope of $-a(p) = (E + 1)/$, so that the insolvency risk of portfolio $P : (E^*, \sigma^*)$ is the β that satisfies $-\phi(\beta) = (E^* + 1)/\sigma^*$, while the insolvency risk of portfolio $G_1(E^R, \sigma^R)$ is the α that satisfies $-\phi(\alpha) = (E^R + 1)/\sigma^R$. Since a larger absolute value of $\phi(\cdot)$ corresponds to a steeper line and to a lower insolvency risk for a chosen portfolio, L^R and L, which are the set of portfolios with a constant probability of insolvency respectively equal to $\alpha > 0$ and $\beta > \alpha$, represent two sets of portfolios with different riskiness (larger on L and lower on L^R). Accordingly, portfolios lying to the right of L have higher insolvency risk than .

Let us consider now, in the Figure 4.2, a regulatory intervention aimed to set a solvency standard, and precisely _ is set as the upper bound of the bank insolvency probability, that is prob $[E \leq -1] \leq \alpha$ or $E \geq -1 - \phi(\alpha)\sigma$. This equation represent the regulator's preference and portfolios on the right of the line L^R, as P_1, do not meet the standard, while the portfolios on the left of L^R are acceptable. Banks whose portfolios are in this part of the graphic are classified as sound, the others are classified as risky.

With the goal to give banks the incentive for achieving, the solvency standard capital regulation can force banks to operate with an equity-to-asset ratio adequate to that standard. In the case illustrated by the figure the adequate level of capital is at least K^R. In fact for each binding $K \geq K^R$ banks are expected to choose G_1 instead of those portfolios on $G_1 G_2$ such as P_1. The requirement $k \geq k^R$ makes the area between $G_1 G_2$ and $G_1 R_2$ infeasible. Nevertheless the constrained efficient frontier is not confined only to $G_0 G_1$, also portfolios on $G_1 R_2$ are feasible. So that the capital ratio requirement is not a sufficient condition to drive banks to the solvency standard. Moreover, any bank with a relative risk aversion parameter $\Gamma < \Gamma'$ which guarantees a portfolio on the global frontier as G_1, would chose a portfolio along $G_1 R_2$, reshuffling its assets towards riskier ones. A lower leverage, forced by capital regulation, may be offset by an increase in business risk.

Then the K-S model points out as the effectiveness of capital ratio regulation when it is a traditional uniform capital ratio regulation, may be impaired in its goal to reduce insolvency risk because of individual bank's preference.

This observation has led Kim and Santomero to analyse in the same framework a capital regulation related to bank riskiness. Since this different constraint to banks' behaviour takes into account individual institutions' preference structure, it should be a more effective way to control the probability of their insolvency.

The risk-related capital regulation suggests, hence, that minimum required levels of bank equity capital depend on the riskiness of asset portfolios where the definition of assets also includes off-balance-sheet items. This schedule can be viewed as an attempt to reduce the implicit increase in deposit insurance exposure associated with the risky banks' asset portfolio choice, which is at least implicitly supported by the insurer and its fixed-rate pricing.

The theoretical form of a risk-related capital regulation can be expressed by:

$$\underline{a}' \underline{X}_1 \leq 1$$

where:

$\underline{a}$ = $n \times 1$ imposed risk weight vector;

$\underline{X}_1$ = $n \times 1$ vector of x_i, that is the ith asset holding, as a proportion of equity capital.

If $\underline{a}$ is correctly set, that is $\underline{a} = \underline{a}^*$. Then a is the minimum amount of equity capital which a bank should hold to back one unit of the ith asset, such that, bounding the probability of insolvency by α, the regulation can be effective in achieving the solvency goal.

In terms of the graphic it means that the capital regulation is effective in making sure that bank operates in the region to the left of the line L^R.

In Figure 4.3 the effects of risk-sensitive capital regulation with theoretically correct risk weights, are described. The aim of this regulation is to drive banks to choose G_1 in its attempt to satisfy $K \geq K^R$, that is it must eliminate the area between $G_1 G_2$ and $G_1 G_3$. The area between $G_1 G_2$ and $G_1 R_2$ is infeasible because of capital regulation $K \geq K^R$, while the area between $G_1 R_2$ and $G_1 G_3$ is eliminated from the opportunity set through adequate risk-weights. The theoretical derivation of such weights goes too far from the aim of this survey of $K - S'$ model. On the contrary it is important to stress the "optimality" aspect of the suggested risk-sensitive capital regulation: to be successful this kind of intervention requires that its sensitiveness to banks' risk be optimal. As for the case of deposit insurance optimality concerns; if the premium has to be set so that to avoid moral hazard effects on banks' behaviour, it must be chosen optimally.

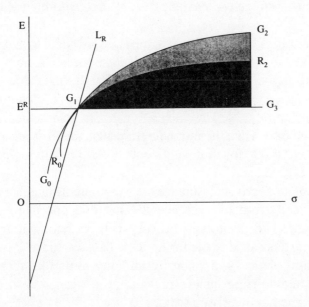

Figure 4.3: The necessary and sufficient condition to bound insolvency risk

4.5 RADICAL ALTERNATIVES

Deposit insurance has perverse effects on banks' behaviour towards risk. Thus it may have a paradoxical outcome on the financial system stability. Many have focused this point- as we have seen – arguing different proposals for reshaping the current insurance systems. Nevertheless any critics and consistent suggestion considered till now, has questioned neither the necessity of deposit insurance nor the fact that it has to be provided by monetary authorities.

Two radical alternatives have removed these foundations arguing for private deposit insurance and for narrow banks.

4.5.1 Private deposit insurance

In current system most of deposit insurance funds are administered by central authorities as well as the managing of the scheme, that is public agencies which have different structure, power and responsibilities in different countries, run deposit insurance interacting within other protection mechanisms and inside regulatory and supervisory policies.

Historical experiences and political issues concerning society's welfare maximization have contributed to set up governmental deposit insurance.

Current difficulties faced by this scheme have led some to support the switch to private administration of deposit insurance.[17] A competitive system appears to be capable of acting efficiently. In a competitive market premiums are expected to be set optimally and the closure rule is expected to be appropriate, not discretional and one which cannot effectively be abused. Then the rationale for private deposit insurance is that it may allow a reduction of government regulation with replacement by market forces.

Some supporters of private insurance have focused the fact that deposit insurance is indeed a form of insurance: the insurer is promising to third party beneficiaries – depositors – that they will be made whole in the event that the parties carrying the insurance – banks – cause them harm by not redeeming deposits. So that by utilizing tools like those with which a profit maximizing insurer protects itself against risk, deposit insurance could be run by private sector.

As we have argued, deposit insurance is not an insurance rather it is a guarantee, since the risk is more a function of the amount of loss suffered in a failure than of the chance of failure. As Horvitz (1983) pointed out, in the case of deposit insurance the identity between risk of bank failure and risk to the insurance system, which characterizes other types of insurance does not exist. Furthermore, in practice, many problems concerning the implementation of an actuarially sound deposit insurance system interpose to a private-provided insurance.

A particularly interesting contribution to how a deposit insurance system might function through a substantial enhancing of private participation has been provided by Campbell and Glenn (1984). They focus on the relationship existing between traditional insurance and governmental deposit insurance in terms of advantages for insured banks, where the relevant variable is the insolvency mechanism inherent in each different system.

Campbell and Glenn's work in fact is founded on the view of deposit insurance system as an alternative legal mechanism for determining when bank insolvency has occurred. The attractiveness of a deposit insurance system depends on the costs associated with the legal mechanism inherent in it where these costs reflect the costs of issuing insured liabilities.

In the case of every kind of firm, including banks, it is difficult to precisely measure when its real net worth falls below zero and then when it becomes insolvent. Market does not value firms assets directly, while it values contingent claims on the firm where the contingency hinges on the legal as well as on the economic definition of insolvency. Thus it is necessary to have some legal procedure for determining when insolvency actually occurs. For most firms other than insured depository institutions, the legal definition has focused on the firm's ability to meet contractual cash-flow obligations. The insolvency mechanism applicable to government insured institutions on the contrary is quite different. The purpose of deposit insurance, in fact, is to eliminate the instability inherent in a system where some banks are highly levered with "instantaneously putable" debt, by subjecting those banks to a particular insolvency legal procedure, unlike the one which applied to other firms. In particular under the deposit insurance system there is a prior commitment between a particular insurer and the insured banks to provide cash when certain contingency is met and such contingency either is defined by some exogenous rule or discretional control over the

145

determination of such contingency is delegated to a responsible third party.

At this point two different kinds of insolvency mechanisms for banks have been selected, the traditional and the deposit insurance system, so that they can be compared to show their respective advantages in terms of costs for banks.

The value of insurance to those who purchase it is determined by the impact of insurance on their costs of issuing debt. Since insurance functions as a substitute for additional equity, additional insurance reduces the cost of debt. Furthermore a private market can be expected to set competitive premiums and the attractiveness of a competitively priced insurance depends on the relative efficiencies of the alternative insolvency mechanisms which are available.

Figure 4.4 illustrates the relevance of costs associated with different bankruptcy systems A and B in determining the attractiveness of insurance. The graph shows the cost of uninsured debt (R_A) for a bank of constant scale as its leverage increases from zero to 1. The cost of debt includes the risk-free interest rate, a risk-premium demanded by the lender and a premium sufficient to cover the expected cost of the relevant insolvency mechanism.

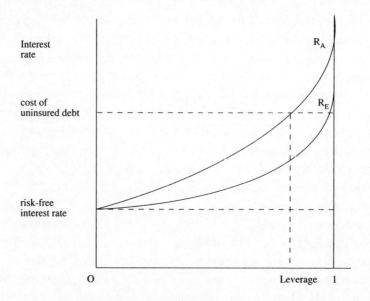

Figure 4.4: Cost associated to different bankcruptcy systems, A and B

Let us consider at first an insolvency mechanism applicable to a bank which is unaffected by the acquisition of insurance on its debt instruments. The value of that insurance, which can be viewed as a private insurance, should be equal to the sum of the risk premium and the premium for insolvency expenses. Since such insurance normally incorporates a liability limit for the guarantor, the price of a unit of insurance coverage should be equal to the cost of debt for a bank with comparable leverage less the risk-free rate, measured in the figure by the difference between curve R and the horizontal line through the risk-free interest rate.

Let now consider the acquisition of an insurance which alters the insolvency mechanism (system B). The cost of debt is altered, in particular it is reduced by the difference in the expected insolvency costs between the private and the governmental system, shifting down the curve of debt cost to R_B. Under this alternative bankruptcy mechanism the competitive price for additional insurance coverage is still equal to the price of debt less the risk-free rate, so that the cost advantages of the alternative insolvency mechanism accrues to banks which utilize insurance.

As Campbell and Glenn stressed, if all relevant markets were unregulated, the two types of insolvency systems might exist simultaneously. Banks that choose to use a high leverage with instantaneous debt might find the cost of the insolvency mechanism implicit in an insurance system more convenient than the traditional alternative, while banks which do not choose to use instantaneously putable debt might view the traditional insolvency mechanism as the least-cost alternative. However, if the insurance is compulsory rather than optional the relationship between insurance system and traditional system costs may be upset, making the former system more expensive than the latter. In this case the costs of deposit system can be offset by subsidizing the system or by other benefits of regulatory framework which accompanies insurance.

This analysis offers a particular outlook over the merits of private versus government deposit insurance. In fact it shifts the emphasis from a comparison based on the insurance nature of the contract between banks and guarantor to a comparison based on the different insolvency mechanism involved in the deposit insurance and in the traditional insolvency system.

This shifting leads us to consider some operation aspects of deposit insurance. The first problem concerns the control over the risk. Government insurance can close a bank in deteriorating condition before its net worth becomes significantly negative, so that public insurer losses can be controlled and its costs are monitoring costs and its risks are measurement errors, rather than risks of bank failure. On the contrary it is not feasible to grant to private deposit insurance companies the right to cancel insurance since a profit maximizing insurer, as the private one, is supposed to cancel insurance if the expected losses from continuing the guarantee exceeded the expected premiums and he will always choose to close the bank earlier rather than late, while in certain circumstances public policy considerations lead to the opportunity to keep some banks operating even though they have negative net worth.

A second problem is, hence, related to the responsibility for the closure rule. An ideal closure rule is one which involves no discretion and one which cannot be effectively abused. Nevertheless the relevance of social costs involved in bank runs gives foundation to the opportunity for discretion responsibilities by the insurer who, then, must be credible, so as solely a public insurer can be. The ability to decide about the perceived magnitude of social costs of closing institutions on large scale, if necessary, and the risk for the financial system are crucial elements of the government deposit insurance. If the private insurer had the discretionary authority to determine when a failure occurred they would be cognizant only of their private cost and not of the social cost of failure.

A further complication rises from the fact that bank solvency depends, to a significant extent, on the willingness of the monetary authorities to provide insured institutions with liquidity, if necessary. If deposit insurance were completely private, presumably private insurers would suppose that liquidity would not be forthcoming to the some extent it would be if the monetary authorities were also responsible for insuring against failure. The potential for this would be reflected in the prices that private insurers would charge. So that the prices at which private insurers could expect to break even could easily be too large to make complete private insurance feasible.

In order to deal with these illiquidity problems it would seem necessary for some public institutions to stand behind any private insurance system and to be ready to inject additional money into it.

Hence derives a role for government at least as a residual guarantor, in order to provide the credibility necessary to avert runs. An operational question is whether this participation by the government in the insurance system can be effectively limited to that of a residual guarantor, that is guarantor of the guarantors.

However, the most important real obstacle facing private deposit insurance focuses on the issue of the social costs of failure. In fact, if the observations concerning the operational aspects to enforce a private deposit insurance which operates with competitive criteria lead to conclude that it is infeasible, observations concerning the social costs of bank failures lead us to conclude that a credible insurance, such a government sponsored one, is desirable.

It is difficult to determine whether social costs of failure should be included in the premiums for insurance, which are charged to insured banks as it would be correct to do in a private system. In fact social costs of a widespread collapse on financial intermediaries are actually costs imposed on society as a whole and therefore it would seem inappropriate to include such costs in premiums, while society should be taxed to cover these costs. Only the sovereign enforcement and taxing power of government is likely to provide the necessary assurance for most banks, so that the aims of deposit insurance can be achieved.

In this view the very approach which supports the idea of a deposit insurance system organized and administered solely by the insured institutions appears inadequate.[18] If it could be satisfactory from the involved banks point of view, it would be inefficient from the point of view of the society. Banks would have no incentives to set a premium greater than their marginal private return, while the society's welfare maximization might imply a greater marginal social return on deposit insurance. This dichotomy may be resolved by the state participation in the scheme.

4.5.2 The narrow banks

The second radical alternative is, in a certain way, more alternative since it envisages restrictions being placed on the use to which insured deposits are put. In particular according to this approach[19] insured deposits may only be invested in a narrow range of low risk assets while more risky activities are being funded from uninsured sources.

This approach, which joins several proposals, supports the adoption of a "safe banking system" that separates banks' deposit taking and payment activities from risky lending. Banks would be limited to safe investment such as governmental securities and highly rated corporate securities, while commercial lending would be carried out by separate entities funded by commercial paper.

The funding for development improving types of lending which are currently done by depositors would have to come from uninsured liabilities issued by the holding companies or its non-depository subsidiaries.

A "narrow banks" proposal advocated by Litan (1987) among others, calls for limiting the set of investments of insured depositories to short-term Treasury bills. In essence, transaction account balances should all be backed 100% by marketable Treasury debt. Narrow banks would be, in the opinion of its advocates, a radical means of achieving many of the reforms proposed for the deposit insurance system, that is, they could introduce market value accounting risk-related net worth standards, risk-related premiums and let the set of regulations drastically revisable.

Guttentag and Herring (1987) have stressed the advantages associated with the introduction of the value of market accounting which is feasible in a split system of financial services. Their proposal, thus, goes beyond the idea that existing depositories should be periodically marked to market. They argue that firms issuing liabilities which include transaction deposits must hold marketable assets and only marketable assets, that is government securities, corporate stocks and bonds, commercial papers and mortgage-backed securities. If depository institutions were structured in such a way, their net worth would be measured every day using current market prices and compared with the institution's required capital, defined ex ante on the basis of the volatility of the portfolio of all the bank's activities. Furthermore, under the proposed system of bank reshaping, an institution's scope for evading capital requirement through off-balance sheet activities, would be sharply limited and deposit insurance would not give the depository institution an incentive to take excessive risk. Capital requirements, in fact, would discipline risk-taking even though creditors would not. Finally, the termination authority would be able to close the depository before it could cause a loss to creditors or the insurer.

The need for a substantial package of back-up supervisory

arrangements and claim on the insurance fund is widely reduced in this de jure split system.

In reality the narrow banks' approach offers an alternative to the regulatory policy rather than an alternative to the deposit insurance system. It substitutes structural reform of the financial service industry for deposit insurance reform, and more than that it outlines a scenario where the need for deposit insurance might become redundant, or as Guttentag and Herring point out "a fail safe, second line of defense". Presumably deposit insurance would be necessary to protect depositors just against cases of outright fraud and theft.

Nevertheless to make banks safe by limiting their activities destroys the important linkage between the deposit-taking and function of banks. If depository institutions were constrained to invest only in government securities or other marketable assets, depositors would be required to sacrifice the economic gains made possible by the existence of financial intermediaries that combine the function of offering both payment services and lending facilities in return for virtually complete safety. Thus the imposition of a narrow bank financial structure would have some undesirable results, first of all the loss of the economy of scope that currently appears exists among depositories' lending and deposit-gathering activities. Hence, the narrow-banks' approach offers a solution to the deposit insurance system's weakness which eliminates its very rationale and together eliminates the fundamental intermediation function of banks, which makes them play an unique role in the economic system.

NOTES

1. See Goodman (1984) on this point.
2. Both principal and interest are guaranteed.
3. For a deep analysis of equation (6) see McKenzie (1989).
4. The shape of a stable distribution is completely determined by its characteristic exponent α, and skewness parameter, β. The characteristic exponent must lie in the interval $(0,2)$ and determines the rate at which the tails of the distribution taper off. The normal distribution is a special case which occurs when α is at its maximum value of 2.
5. When $\alpha > 2$ the distribution has paretian tails that behave asymptotically like a Pareto distribution and which are longer than the tails of normal distribution. This means that the probability of an event well out in tail of distribution depends crucially on the value of α. Furthermore if $\beta = 0$ the distribution is

symmetrical. Two more parameters characterize paretian distribution used by McCulloch, C, the scale parameter that contracts or expand the distribution and p, the location parameter that is the mean of the distribution.

6. If $\alpha = 2$, then $\sin(\pi\alpha/2) = 0$, therefore $\lambda = 0$ and there are no discontinuities in net worth.

7. See Merrick and Saunders (1985).

8. $p^*(\cdot)$ and $e^*(\cdot)$ are derived in Chan-Mak model as optimal solution functions.

9. Kanatas refers to Fdic arrangements where there exist insured and uninsured deposits. See Chapter 1.

10. Recall that an increase in α_1 (insurance premium on risky loans) raises the probability of bankruptcy of firm j and marginally lowers the resale value of A.

11. See Goodman (1984).

12. This issue has been pointed out by Carns (1989).

13. This has been the case in the early 1980s when Penn Square National Bank of Oklaoma's uninsured depositors perceived a market change. Since it was disposed to deal with that bank through a deposit payout rather than a merger, uninsured depositors ran quickly creating temporary funding problems also to other banks with whom credit lines and loan participation existed. This event required considerable discount window assistance.

14. Sharpe considers three balance sheets at time t, bank's, insurer's and depositors', where all amounts are economic values. Bank has assets (A_t) and claims an assets (D_t, C_t). Since there is some risk that the bank may not pay its depositors claims D_t, in full and on time, the economic value of such claims is less than it would be if there were no such risk. So that insured depositors have claims on the bank D_t and claims on the insurer $(D_{Ft} - D_t)$ and a net worth equal to D_{Ft} since they consider their claims default-free. The insurer has liabilities to depositors equal to $(D_{Ft} - D_t) = L_t$, and its net worth depends on the reserves that insurance premium brings in.

15. Kim and Santomero model assumptions are: a) banks are price takers in their respective markets; b) a bank holds n assets and one deposit item the return of which have a joint normal distribution. The ith asset has expected return u_i and variance σ_i^2. The deposit has expected cost u_0 and variance σ_0^2; c) banks are single-period risk-averse expected utility maximizers. The utility function is approximated by the first and second moments of the final wealth. Thus, the bank's strictly quasi-concave objective function U is definited over mean, E, and standard deviation, σ, of return on equity capital. The risk preference is measured by the relative risk aversion parameter Γ; d) Bank regulators are interested in a "safe and sound" banking system and hence try to bound the probability of bank insolvency through capital adequacy requirements.

16. The portfolio choice of the bank from an identified opportunity set depends on its utility function $U(E, \sigma)$. This function guarantees a unique solution to this choice which is determined by equating the bank's marginal rate of substitution between return and risk to the marginal rate of transformation along the derived efficient frontier.

152

17. Ely (1985) supported this idea by proposing a system where industry cross-guarantees would make banks themselves provide the depositor protection.
18. McCarthy (1980).
19. Litan (1987) provided this alternative for reforming deposit insurance.

5 Comparative analysis of deposit insurance schemes

The foregoing analysis has focused on the theoretical aspects of deposit insurance and its interrelations with banks' behaviour.

Our referent deposit insurance scheme has been that of U.S.A., because of its long operating experience and because it has been the most questioned and assessed by the economic literature. Nonetheless other different schemes work in many financial systems. They have various characteristics, different structures and probably related to their particular way of operating it is the role single monetary authorities have assigned to them.

From the following survey, hence, it is expected to get a greater insight into deposit insurance issue, especially with regard to those contradictory aspects which theory has pointed out but finally left wavering. Practical solutions adopted by different countries to protect deposits can offer some suggestions which pass over those of Fdic case and which bring more knowledge elements.

Moreover, since the different deposit insurance schemes have been introduced after the pioneering U.S. experience and they are differently dated over time, it is presumable that even though they have been established with the some main purpose to ensure the financial stability of the economic system, they pursue their aim differently and pursue more than one intermediate objective.

As we have seen the rationale for deposit insurance is not univocal. Evolution in banking industry, the securitization process which affected it[1] and its increasing international interdependence has given relevance to further issues concerning the financial stability. Together with the small depositors protection and the control over the event of bank runs, the necessity to preserve the payment system from systemic crises has entered the spectrum of deposit insurance aims. In this way causes and effects of instability have no more circumscribed outline and they are no more immutable. The development of the banking industry changes the involved risks, the objective of monetary policy shifts and its instruments are to be fitted.

Most countries have introduced their deposit protection schemes after an event with shaking consequences on the financial system or whose effects could have been potentially damaging for the financial stability. The preservation of depositors' confidence in the institutions has hence been the crucial motive for deposit insurance establishment.

In the nineteenth century local panics led many states of America to establish formal system of deposit insurance.[2] The experience of the state schemes was mixed and depending upon the strength of the crises those schemes were facing they were successful or unsuccessful. In the twentieth centuries clearinghouses protection role – according with the structural evolution of financial systems – has been replaced by central banks increasing involvement in the managing of the monetary stability through the lender of last resort function. However in many countries the exigence arose to overcome the discretion in central banks' intervention during crises and then to reduce the likelihood of collapse from misassessment and mismanagement of bank troubles as occurred in 1929 with the inadequate intervention of the Fed in the American market. Moreover, the establishment of a separate institutional fund solely intended to stand by, allowed central banks to preserve their "super partes" role, without being directly involved in single bank failures. On the other hand a direct or indirect intensification in supervision of depository institutions could be achieved.

Then the actual structures of the various deposit insurance schemes show the traces of those functions they were expected to undertake within the financial system widely framed and already settled. Whether the scheme is privately or officially run, what is the degree of government subsidy, what are the levels of cover and premiums are issues that do not concern formal aspects for a deposit insurance programme. They are substantial elements which give relevance to different political choices. These choices are crucial for a bank's competitive edge in an increasing international dimension for the financial systems.

The following sections discuss the present deposits insurance schemes in order to focus their differences and the similarities, and to investigate their effectiveness. Since each scheme depends upon the characteristics of the financial system they operate within, we will try to give adequate relevance to these relationships. However our straight aim in this chapter is to consider the most significant schemes and their main features summarizing almost the existing in a synoptic table (see page 178).[3]

5.1 NON EUROPEAN COUNTRIES GROUP OF TEN MEMBERS

5.1.1 United States

The federal deposit insurance programme was instituted in 1934 in the aftermath of the collapse of some thousand banks in the previous three years of the great depression.

The American experience, excluding the previous clearinghouses', is the first example all over the world of direct deposit protection on a legal basis.

The Fdic was, in fact, duly established to help supervise and provide deposit insurance to banks, with the Federal Home Loan Bank Board (Fhlbb), through its insurance arm – Fslic – and the National Credit Union Share Insurance Fund performing the same duties in respect of savings and loan associations, some federal savings banks and credit unions respectively.

Until 1982 the Fdic's insurance activity embraced only commercial banks and state-chartered mutual savings banks. In 1982 the Garn St-German Depository Institutions Act added a new category of banks to Fdic competence, those mutual savings banks which elected not to change their insurance agency on switching to a federal charter. The Financial Institution Reform, Recovery and Enforcement Act in 1989 transferred to Fdic also the insurance responsibilities of Fhlbb because Fslic became insolvent.

Therefore, since 1989 the Fdic is responsible for the administration of deposit insurance for virtually the whole of the U.S. deposit-taking sector. This function is provided through the medium of the new Bank Insurance Fund (Bif) and the Savings Association Insurance Fund (Saif) for commercial banks and s&l's respectively.

The participation in Fdic is compulsory for member banks, that is for banks which are part of the Fed, and it is voluntary for other institutions.

The main characteristic of the American deposit protection programme is that Fdic is not just charged to make depositors safer through the reimbursement of their funds, rather it performs some fundamental supervision duties for the banking industry.

The other schemes existing in different countries very seldom combine these two functions under the responsibility of a unique authority. Many operate in close connection with central banks and other monetary institutions, but their control powers on those banks which receive protection are usually limited to the duration of some sound conditions to continue protecting their deposits.

The supervision activity of the Fdic is large. The Fdic is responsible for the supervision and regulation of all insured banks which are not members of the Fed, and of chartered insured branches of foreign banks. Two agencies associated to the Fdic, the Office of the Comptroller of the Currency and the Board of Governors of the Federal Reserve System, on the other hand, examine National Banks, federal and state banks and the branches of foreign banks which are not insured. However in this case the Fdic supervises the final reports of the two agencies.

Through its supervision activities, the Fdic determines single institution situation according to the Uniform Interagency Bank Rating System, known as Camel. Each institution receives a rating, from 1 to 5, for five areas, capital, assets, management, earnings and liquidity as well as a composite rating reflecting the examiner's overall assessment. Related to different Camel rates the Fdic can intervene with four types of actions: the denial of insurance, the termination of insured *status*, the cease and desist order, the suspension and removal of directors and officers.

The Fdic also provides monitoring of banks every three months through the call reports. A statistical system allows banks to divide into different classes, in order to identify those in serious trouble and in order to supply depositors, banks and examiners with useful information about banks' situations.

While as supervisor the Fdic performs a preventive activity to avoid banks falling into crisis, as an insurer the Fdic may intervene to limit effects of illiquidity or insolvency crises or paying off depositors. When a bank is declared insolvent from the chartering authorities the pay off procedure is intended to reimburse depositors up to the limit of $100,000.[4] Depositors holding accounts at the domestic offices of an insured institutions receive complete protection up to this level. The coverage is applied on a per customer per bank basis. The Fdic, after depositors pay-off, liquidates the bank's assets as receiver and distributes funds to uninsured creditors, including proportionate payments to itself for the amount that it has advanced. If collections on assets ultimately exceed liabilities, then all creditors will receive the full amount of their claims plus interest.

Ever since their introduction, federal deposit insurance premiums to fund the scheme have always been levied on a flat rate basis as a percentage of the assessable deposits. This percentage currently[5] is set at the rate of 12 basis points – 12 cents per $100 -for contributors to Bif, whilst contributors to Saif pay a rate of 20.8 basis point.[6] Fund contributors are entitled to rebates if the funds exceed a certain size. Since 1984 the Fdic operates with its funds; any possibilities of borrowing from the Treasury are excluded, except for a special emergency withdrawal of 3 billion dollars.

The pay off procedure is the most straightforward option for the Fdic. Nevertheless it is also the most costly and disruptive of banking services, so that Fdic has often opted to avoid the pay-off of large banks. Among the different arrangements Fdic may opt for is this solution – so-called modified pay-off. It is the most similar to an insurance reimbursement because it arrives after the bank failure.

Under the modified pay-off, insured depositors receive full payments and large depositors receive partial payments on the insured portions of their deposits ; the partial payments are based on an Fdic estimate of the proceeds from the liquidation of the assets of the failed bank. If recoveries on the assets eventually exceed the initial estimate, the uninsured depositors receive additional payment; if the proceeds from liquidating those assets fall short of the partial payment, the Fdic absorbs the loss.

The partial payment disrupts the activities of uninsured depositors less than the traditional deposit pay-off does. In some cases handled under the modified pay-off procedure, the Fdic arranges for another bank to assume only the insured deposits of a failed bank.

The acquiring bank pays a premium which reduces losses and the acquired bank's office generally remains open. The acquiring bank may be an institution established temporarily up to two years; insured deposits are transferred to this bank and Fdic provides for its liquidity needs. At the end of the two years the bridge-bank may be sold or liquidated.

According to the modified pay-off uninsured depositors suffer a loss that, in economic impact, is somewhat less than some of their uninsured funds. This solution, if followed consistently would tend to encourage market discipline. But, by its very nature, market discipline, so far as depositors are concerned, means an increased tendency toward bank runs and instability.

If banking industry stability greatly concerns, the Fdic can arrange other procedures which also save the direct costs of a pay-off and are intended to preserve the going-concern value of the failed bank.

If there is a virtual interest by other banks in acquiring the failed bank and there are not circumstances, such as contingent liabilities, which make it difficult to estimate losses, the Fdic tends to use the purchase and assumption method. In the P&A transaction, all failed bank's deposit liabilities are assumed by another bank, which also purchases some of the failed bank's assets.

The Fdic initiates a P&A transaction by soliciting bids from other banks, bank holding companies or individuals, for the purchase of assets and the assumption of deposit liabilities. The acquiring bank must assume all deposit liabilities and acquire assets considered to be of good value, excluding loans and debt instruments that are not likely to be paid in full.[7] Additional cash will be provided by the Fdic if the value of the assets offered for the purchase is less than deposit liabilities to be assumed.

The P&A transactions are used to prevent disruption of banking services when the bank has a book of continuing business or customer good-will which will contribute to profit in the future. Furthermore, since entry into banking is restricted, the bank charter itself has economic value and the acquiring bank acquires something more than the failed bank value.

This type of the Fdic intervention gives uninsured depositors the impression that they are not exposed to risk of loss when their bank fails. As a consequence, they would not attempt to restraint the risk assumed by their banks destroying market discipline. However, in some cases, it appears appropriate to privilege considerations about the resulting impact on public confidence rather than on market discipline.

In the light of these arguments other procedures are adopted by the Fdic to handle problem banks, so that apart from the de jure protection received, depositors enjoy additional benefits. Under certain circumstances, the Fdic is authorized to make loans to failing banks, or purchase assets from them. Until the Gar-St. German Act, the Fdic was limited to the use of the direct assistance only where the continued existence of the failing bank was essential to its community. Now the Fdic is allowed to provide assistance to a keep a bank in operation when that is the least costly option available.

This procedure[8] implies that the Fdic will take over and temporarily manage the problem bank or the insolvent institution with a view to restructuring it and selling it in the future. All depositors are made safe by this procedure, but its effects on market discipline are ruinous: with depositors also the bank shareholders and management are protected. In this sense the direct assistance the Fdic may provide is beyond its insurance duties. It concerns more closely the Fdic supervision responsibility on insured banks, since the direct assistance intervention occurs before the bank failure and any reimbursement is made.

Although it was planned and established as a deposit insurance scheme, intended to protect small depositors in the event of bank failure, the american system has resulted in operating in quite a different manner. The actual failure resolution policies adopted by the Fdic and its increased involvement in banking industry control, have supported its development towards a hybrid nature.

The continuous necessity to balance social and private costs, the often fearful behaviour of Fdic and its being overly concerned with political consequences of imposing significant losses on customers of failing banks, have in more than half century caused the scheme to depart from its original rationale. Furthermore, the evolution of the financial system where it was intended to operate presumably have changed the game rules, changing also its referent environment.

That is why, although it is structured as an insurance, literature is focused on its possible reforms to limit its present distortive effects and its troubles. However many other systems, born successively, have been capable of profiting by the Fdic incomparable and seminal experience.

5.1.2 Canada

The Cdic, the Canadian Deposit Insurance Corporation, was set up in 1967, together with Qdib, the Quebec Deposit Insurance Board, which guarantees deposits within the province of Quebec.

These funds, whose membership is mandatory for all federally incorporated institutions are aimed at protecting small depositors. In fact, any deposit, including term deposits up to five years and debentures in Canadian currency payable in Canada and held by any legal person, are covered up to 60,000 Canadian dollars. Moreover, deposits under registered home ownership schemes, registered retirement plants and joint deposits count as separate deposits of the same person.

The Cdic fund is unique for banks, trust companies and mortgage loan companies and its interventions are for acquiring assets from member institutions in trouble, making loans or advances to them and placing deposits with them.

The involvement of the deposit insurance scheme in insured banks activity is relatively high. In fact Cdic carries out examination and supervision activities on member institutions but although its discretionary powers to terminate the insurance of an institution operating unsatisfactorily, it may not close down an insolvent institution on its own initiative.

Members are charged a 33 per mill of insured deposit annual premium, which can be reduced if the Cdic considers the fund as adequate. Finally the fund may borrow from the government.

5.1.3 Japan

In 1971 the Deposit Insurance Corporation was established on the initiative of the Bank of Japan, whose vice-governor is also managing director of the Dic. However private financial organizations participate in running the insurance fund through their membership in the Dic working committee.

Deposits are paid off up to 3 million yen and member banks, trust banks, long-term credit co-operatives contribute to the fund with a 0.12 per mill of insured deposits premiums, without the possibility of any reduction, rebate or addition in the occurrence of insured event such as suspension of deposit withdrawals or cancellation of licence.

The central bank, which contributed for one third of the initial fund capital, is operative as lender to the fund. Nevertheless, differently from most cases of deposit insurance, the Japanese scheme do not consider surveillance and control activities of the Dic on member banks, even if recently some standard – as a minimum capital/assets ratio and maximum in bank exposure to a single borrower – has been introduced that banks have to comply with.

5.2 EEC COUNTRIES

The Commission of EEC took interest with deposit protection issue during the '70s. The proposals dated back to those years showed an ambitious programme intended to call all member states to place in their financial systems a deposit-guarantee scheme with a minimum coverage protecting deposits of all banks except interbank deposits. Furthermore the various European schemes were viewed as supported by a solidarity among all of them in order to provide, in the event of particularly serious crises, a virtual Community-wide protection system.

However any proposals exited the embryo stage up to 1984. In the meanwhile since some countries had introduced their schemes or were going to do that, the Community effort was aimed not only at introducing some new protection procedures, but also to harmonize those existing ones.

The goal focused on by the Community was principally that of the handling of a problem credit institution on the brink of failure. The issue of deposit insurance therefore became consequential.

The proposal for a Council Directive formulated in 1984 and submitted to the Council on 1986,[9] was intended to coordinate laws, regulations and administrative provisions relating to the reorganization and winding-up of credit institutions.

The principle stated by the proposal was that of stimulating wider procedures of intervention during the stage before the insolvency of a banking firm. On the other hand, the need to consider depositors' interest in having their savings protected oriented the Community to consider explicitly in the title iv of the proposal (art.16) the establishment of deposit insurance schemes or their improvement.

Member states which had already set up a deposit guarantee are called to ensure that their schemes, operative in their territory, cover the deposits of branches of institutions having their head office in another member state.

In those states where the entry in force of a deposit guarantee scheme is pending, are called to ensure that the deposit-guarantee schemes – in which the institutions that have their head office in their territory take part – extend cover to deposits received by branches set up in host countries within the Community which have no deposit-guarantee scheme, under the same condition as those laid down to guarantee deposits received in the home country.

The final objective of the proposal, hence, was to provide the same protection over the Community: it is unacceptable and contrary to the Treaty to have as consequence of a bank failure deposits differently protected, or not protected at all, in the same EEC territory.

At the end of 1986 a Commission Recommendation[10] was addressed to promote the introduction of deposit-guarantee schemes all over the Community. Six member states still had no deposit-guarantee schemes and the Commission aimed at safeguarding the existing initiative and at promoting further them, both private and governmental. Hereby the Commission Recommendation was three-fold, according to three different cases.

In the first case, the Commission recommended that member states which already had one or more deposit-guarantee schemes – Belgium, the Federal Republic of Germany, Spain, France, the Netherlands and the United Kingdom – should have checked in the event of the winding-up of credit institutions revealing insufficient assets, that those schemes:

- guaranteed compensation for small depositors (unsophisticated savers);
- covered the depositors of all authorized credit institutions;
- distinguished sufficiently and clearly between intervention prior to the winding-up and compensation after winding-up;
- clearly set up the criteria for compensation and the formalities to be completed in order to receive compensation.

This part of the Recommendation, then, was aimed to set some fundamental common features in the existing schemes.

The second case concerned the member states which already had plans for introducing deposit-guarantee schemes – Italy, Ireland and Portugal. They were recommended to check that their plans met the conditions determined for the first group of countries and, furthermore, they were recommended to take all the appropriate measures to ensure that their schemes were adopted by 31 December 1988.

This provision was intended to fix a time limit for the extension of deposit guarantee in all member states. Consequently the third part of the recommendations was addressed to those states which did not have a deposit-guarantee system covering all their institutions and which did not have drawn up plans for such a scheme, namely, Denmark, Greece and Luxembourg. They were recommended to draw up a plan and to take all appropriate measures to ensure that planned schemes came in force by 1 January 1990.

At the present, following the mentioned recommendation, all member states except Greece and Portugal have deposit protection schemes in place, and these two countries are planning to introduce deposit protection arrangements shortly.

The Commission is preparing a legally-binding directive setting minimum standards for deposit-guarantee provisions and plans to produce a draft directive in the first half of 1992.

The present Commission aim is to provide effective deposit-guarantee arrangements for individual depositors while ensuring that deposit-guarantee provisions do not themselves become part of the problem by encouraging customers to place funds imprudently and banks to take excessive risks.

The Commission is also pressing forward with work to harmonize the legal provision applying to banks in difficulty to avoid defaults being triggered by differences in national legal practice.

One important change the planned Deposit Guarantee Directive will make is to move deposit-guarantee protection from a host-country to a home-country basis. The member state responsible for the overall prudential control of a bank should also bear the responsibility of providing the resources to fund the deposit-guarantee provision if things go wrong.

With this drawback concerning EEC orientations towards deposit protection, the following survey will outline the main European schemes, that is those which are pioneers in the European experience or which present special operative framework.

5.2.1 United Kingdom

Over the period 1973–74 the U.K. experienced a wide banking crisis and tested the ability of the Bank of England to respond to this crisis organizing a support operation, the so called "life-boat fund", with the aid of funds from large multi-branch domestic clearing banks. This co-operative fund operated identifying problem banks and, where feasible, gave support by re-cycling deposits or making short-term loans. The risks of this operation were shared on an agreed formula based on clearing bank size.

The life-boat operation was successful: in the first year more than 1,200 million pounds were extended in loans to 26 problem banks and public confidence in the banking system was restored. Nevertheless the success of this type of government-private sector co-operative bail out did not reduced the incentive to established a mechanism for extinguishing single banking institutions when insolvent and inefficient. On the contrary it can be argued it was the spark for the present deposit insurance.

Small savers protection did not seem to be reliably achievable through occasional agreements between the Bank of England and the clearing banks. The life-boat operation had been effective in restoring depositors' confidence but presumable this had occurred as far as the confidence of large depositors was concerned.[11] Furthermore it appeared important to give the central bank an official device to pay off depositors in the event of a bank insolvency.

Together with a more active and forestalling role which the Bank of England had been assuming during crisis events, the establishment of a deposit insurance was also viewed as a mechanism to support the system with liquidity if necessary.

However the settlement of the Deposit Protection Board in 1982 – under the provision of the Banking Act of 1979 – did not exclude the direct intervention of the central bank during a crisis. Since the co-operative experience worked so well it appeared that it could provide a format for action in relatively concentrated banking systems. Then the deposit insurance plan, while aimed at pursuing a risk-sharing approach to future banking crises, virtually was conceived to guarantee that in the event of a bank failure large depositors came to rely on the intervention of the Bank of England through some new life-boat operations to protect their deposits.

Differently from analogous experiences – as the case of Italy for example – the establishment of deposit insurance in England was part of a wider banking industry reform. The Banking Act of 1979, in fact, which provided in its second part (arts. 21-33) a compulsory deposit insurance scheme was principally aimed at introducing a supervision system over banking activities that until then had not been subject to any regulation law. So that deposit insurance was conceived as an instrument complementary to the surveillance, supervision and control of the banking system performed by the central bank.

In this insight the Deposit Protection Board was established in 1982 to run – under the administration of the Bank of England – an insurance fund which covers recognized banks and licensed deposit taking institutions. Since the public institutions, as the National Saving Bank and the National Girobank, already had their deposits guaranteed by the Treasury and the Building Societies were protected by a voluntary Investor Protection Scheme, the protection of other banks came to complete the system wide security net for small savers.

According to this view it is the provision for branches and subsidiaries of foreign banks to be excluded from the protection if the Board is satisfied that sterling deposits at their U.K. offices are as well protected by the scheme in the countries of origin as they would be by the U.K. scheme.

Since the explicit goal of the U.K. deposit insurance scheme is the protection of small savers, protected depositors are selected according to this objective and hence not all depositors are guaranteed. Resident and not resident depositors, also if they are small companies with simple financial structures, have their sterling deposits with U.K. offices of an institution protected with maximum amount of 20,000 pounds. Secured deposits with an original maturity of more than five years and certificates of deposits are excluded. Furthermore interbank deposits, deposits of companies or persons (families and managers) involved in the banking institution which failed are excluded.

Together with small protection aim, the U.K. deposit insurance scheme was conceived to cause limited effects on depositors discipline towards bank behaviour. Thus a coinsurance mechanism has been introduced into the scheme, according to which only three-quarters of the amount of the protected deposits are payable after the insolvency of the institution. Then, in the event of a bank failure, eligible depositors will receive 75% of the first 20,000 pounds.

The rationale for U.K. deposit insurance fund is to maintain the fund's resources constant and then the fund's capacity to intervene. So that bank's contributions, which are in normal conditions only initial contributions, have to bring the fund up to £5-6 million as stated by the Board. In 1982 the recognized or licensed banks paid out their contributions of 0.02 per cent of their average deposit base with a minimum single contribution of £2,500 and a maximum of £300,000. Subsequently, all banks which are recognized or licensed, which then become eligible, pay out a minimum contribution- currently equal to £10,000 – since they have not yet any deposits.

Apart from new admissions, further contributions of member banks may be levied to bring the fund back to between £5 and £6 million if at the end of the financial year it falls below £3 million. If it appears that payments in any financial year are likely to exhaust the fund, special contributions may be levied to meet the commitments of the fund. These contributions, which have no limits in their amounts – if not the 0,3 per cent of single bank deposit base – are the principal guarantee for the U.K. scheme together with the fund's power to borrow up to £10 million on temporary basis. Finally, extraordinary payments are provided according to the Treasury power to increase permanently fund liquidity over the £5-6 million ceiling.

The U.K. deposit insurance scheme, hence, works as a device aimed to redistribute costs of bank failures among actors of the banking industry in order to rid society of them. In this insight Deposit Protection Board powers are limited. The central bank, when an institution is becoming insolvent, may decide to let that institution fail without any intervention, to intervene in favour of small depositors and finally to gather liquid funds and support temporary the trouble bank until it becomes again sounds.

The second choice involves the deposit insurance scheme thereby the board which is charged to pay off depositors and to substitute creditors of the failed bank. Realization of failed bank assets is then employed to reimburse the fund, residual depositors' losses and member banks if they have paid special contributions to the fund. However, the central bank still retains the residual ability to enforce market discipline on large depositors and the banking system by choosing which banks support, and by how much, with co-operative loans.

5.2.2 Italy

The Italian deposit protection scheme differs from previous and from many other schemes in that it operates within an articulated safety net where a central role is played by the Bank of Italy as banking supervisor.

The scheme is not autonomous and actually independent and, above all, its interventions are not automatic. While there exists inside the protection system a fund for the protection of deposits so that an explicit scheme is established, the fund interventions are triggered by a process that involves the whole of the safety net. Furthermore, since the establishment of the Fondo Interbancario di Tutela dei Depositi (Fitd) in 1986 has been included in the existing protection system without reshaping it, at the present, different instruments exist which pursue the same aim.

The Banking Law, passed in 1936 and subsequently modified, provides a structure in which the savings that flow into the banks are indirectly protected by a system of controls and considers different solutions for problem banks which are aimed at keeping a bank in operation or, if that proves impossible, to preserve their organizational and operational structure, minimizing social costs of a failure.

In particular two legal procedures are available to handling bank crises: extraordinary administration and compulsory administrative liquidation. Whichever procedure is adopted depends upon the seriousness of the crisis. However both them are initiated at the request of the Bank of Italy by a decree issued by the Minister of the Treasury. The Governor of the Bank of Italy is entrusted with the appointment of the extraordinary commissioners and of the liquidators and the central bank is responsible for supervising the application of the procedures. The two procedures are only alternatives in a formal sense; in practice they are in sequence. The compulsory liquidation is one of the possible outcomes of extraordinary administration. In fact, the latter is aimed at taking over and temporarily (last for up to eighteen months) handling the problem bank in order to identify the causes of the crisis and the best way to overcome it. The bank goodwill may persuade shareholders or, more often, third parties to provide new equity capital.

Compulsory administrative liquidation is a legal method which takes the place of the ordinary bankruptcy procedure in banks. This procedure makes the failed bank exit the market under the supervision of the central monetary authorities. In fact the liquidator is appointed by the Governor of the Bank of Italy and the latter's supervision of the application of the procedure allows the exercise of technical skills so as to liquidate assets as rapidly and advantageously as possible.

Beside these methods of resolving banking crises, other alternative devices are provided by the Italian law in order to protect depositors: the merger of the failed bank into a sound one or the transfer of assets and liabilities to an other institution, as in a Fdic's P&A operation. In practice, in this last case another bank replaces the bank being wound up in the running of its branches. This bank immediately takes over the liabilities and subsequently acquires all or part of assets when their value has been agreed with the liquidators.

In the takeover procedure, which usually occurs for large crises, the involved bank is supported by the Bank of Italy under the provision of the "Sindona decree".[12] The value of the failed bank assets even when the value of the goodwill is added, is more likely less than that of liabilities which consist mainly of deposits. Then the Bank of Italy enables the bank involved to enter into the operation by granting its advances at subsidizing interest rates. When these are invested at market rates the interest differential enables the loss incurred in the takeover to be gradually made good.

The mentioned apparatus to resolve a banking crisis appears to be articulated and complex. It is founded on the central bank authority in handling financial system also in its pathological experiences and it is aimed to spread the negative effects of a bank failure over other parts of the financial system through the support of the community.

On the other hand the available devices show a wide degree of discretion in the choice of the different procedures to adopt and the protection system as a whole is founded on central bank lending function which provides an indirect protection of deposits.

Thus, when in 1986 the Fitd was set up, it was not conceived to be an alternative to the existing system being aimed, according to its statute, at providing a "further" protection for members' deposit accounts.

Although the U.S. Fdic has been a referent, the Italian choice towards deposit insurance has been quite different. The Fitd, in fact, is a voluntary consortium among banking institutions and differs from other protection funds in that its members are almost all credit institutions. Further it has private nature, albeit the Bank of Italy has an extensive role in controlling and managing it and its interventions are strictly subject to monetary authorities.

These features give the Italian fund an ambiguous nature settled between insurance and mutual assistance. On one hand the extensive participation in the fund of different categories of institutions, including also the Italian branches of the foreign banks, is a response to a solidarity aim; on the other hand, the fund is a deposit insurance in that it shifts the costs of bank failure from the community to the banking industry, it has some operating autonomy and, in certain cases, undertakes payoff procedures.

As for the Fdic, once a bank crisis occurred, the Fitd has different alternative ways to intervene, as provided by its statute.

If it is the case of a bank failure the fund pays off deposits and becomes creditor of the failed institution. Deposits up to 200 million lire are completely protected; up to 800 million lire they are protected at 75 per cent and for the part exceeding 1 billion lire they have no protection. Interbank deposits, deposits of savers involved in bank administration and deposits which received a particularly high rate of interest are excluded by the pay off procedure.

Alternatively to the pay-off procedure, the Fitd may intervene promoting a bridge-bank operation, according to the liquidator and with the central bank authorization.

If it is the case for the extraordinary administration the fund Committee may arrange – whereas it is the cheapest solution – a direct assistance to the problem bank through other members lending, guarantees from other external bank or other kind of intervention as authorized by Fitd Council.

A particular feature of the Italian fund concerns the contributions of participating institutions. In fact they are on call so that the fund is actually a virtual one and members are called upon to contribute just in case of a fund intervention. In this way unnecessary resources locked up in the fund are avoided. The single contributions, which differ from one another, are fixed in their total amount. They have to bring into the fund 1 per cent of members' total deposits up to the limit of 4,000 billion lire. The amount may be increased any time up to the exposure of the fund and with a limit of 0.05 per cent of the total deposits.

Single members quotas are set according to their respective contribution basis and according to a regressive criterion. Each member institution, hence, contributes to the fund in accordance to its potentialities which are under the control of the Fitd through the imposition of certain standards respect, under pain of exclusion from the consortium.

The last peculiar characteristic of the Italian fund is that there is no possibility to borrow from the central bank to finance its intervention. It is a direct consequence of the role the Fitd plays within the protection system where other devices are available which involve central bank lending functions.

5.2.3 France

Similar to the Italian system is, in a certain way, the French deposit protection scheme. In fact a voluntary and virtual system for commercial banks exists which may intervene in problem members also through rescuing operations. Though their structures are similar, nevertheless their imprinting is quite different.

While the system operating in Italy is conceived to be between a solidarity fund and an insurance fund, the french scheme is explicitly aimed at pursuing the assistance of member banks; a solidarity goal which is founded on a wide-spread concept of "banking community" and on a strong corporative spirit of the bank institutions.

The deep moral group sense of the French banking industry has widely characterized its history and its configuration.

The Banking Law of 1984 has introduced regulation and control forms applying to all credit institutions and reshaped the control authorities. Nevertheless it has at the same time officially sanctioned the role of the Association Française des Banques (Afb) to which all banks are expected to be associated directly or indirectly. Thus a corporative organization has come to take on an institutional function within the financial system.

In this prospective back to the 1980 a mechanism of "professional solidarity" was established, run by the Afb and without any legal or statutory foundation and furthermore completely independent from monetary authorities.

It is not the case for a guarantee fund because member banks are called automatically to underwrite when an event of bank failure occurs such funds to meet the problem bank needs. The mechanism of solidarity in this protection scheme corresponds, therefore, to a drawing right of the Afb on its members. Calls for contributions cannot be larger than 100 million francs during one year, even if past contributions, back to two years before, and future contribution, up to two years to come, can be called so that the yearly global interventions of the system can amount up to 500 million francs. If pay-off operations are undertaken – it arrives only when problem bank rescue is impossible – depositors are reimbursed up to the limit of 400,000 francs. Interbank deposits, foreign currency deposits, bearer deposits, deposits of person involved in the failed bank activity, deposits excessively remunerated and, finally, deposits of french banks abroad are excluded from pay-off procedures.

Member bank contributions are calculated according to a complex scheme founded on regressive and progressive criteria respectively with the increasing amount of deposits and with the increasing size of the intervention.

The mentioned scheme operates for commercial banks. Other categories of institutions have their depositor protection schemes, differently arranged according to their aim. Some of them are prevention mechanism, some others are more closed to insurance schemes protecting directly the depositors of failed banks.

The French system of deposit protection is then articulated and it works within a banking framework where legislation provides also mechanisms of control, surveillance and therefore, of indirect protection. These mechanisms have been set up in particular because of the extensive presence of the State in the banking system. Massive successive nationalization measures, in fact, have spread public protection over the banking industry: at the beginning of the '80s due to the interbank sharing nearly the whole of the banking system arrived at being controlled by public power. So that when the Afb protection programme was established in 1980 it was actually aimed at protecting small and medium sized banks which are mostly private banks.

The public-private composition of French banking industry and the presence of a security system where supremacy of the State and professional solidarity incentives blended, have made french experience unique. Nevertheless, a process has been triggered to achieve a greater certainty in handling banking crises and it is aimed at overcoming the lack of enunciated rules and the wide discretion to manage bank failures is the provision of the 1984 Banking Law (art.52) of a special central bank intervention. According with this provision the Governor may invite – if the situation requires it – the shareholders of problem institution to provide the necessary support, and he may also arrange an agreement among credit institutions to protect deposits and third parties, ensuring credibility of the financial system. This provision places beside the discretion of Afb in handling commercial banks failures a chance for central bank intervention, by reinforcing institutional aspects of deposit guarantee system.

5.2.4 Germany

The contemporary presence of different schemes which provide certain guarantees to depositors, characterizes also the German banking industry. Nevertheless these schemes operate within a financial system widely market oriented, where an institutional deposit protection programme has not had foundations to be established.

Devices for the maintenance of the financial stability exist within the German banking system, but they are conceived to ensure the respect of the market forces and of the competition criteria. The Banking Law of 1961, in fact, provided instruments to avoid bank failures which were limited to the preventive surveillance of institutions from the Bundesbank and successive laws were oriented to reinforce the surveillance activities of the monetary authorities. This in particular was the case of the law passed in 1976 and of that passed in 1984. The latter introduced capital requirements and restrictions to large lending operations in order to maintain a free structure of the banking market together with some regulations.

This environment has stimulated spontaneous agreements arranged by the three principal German bank categories: commercial banks, savings banks and co-operative banks. These agreements, though not legalized, were favoured by the law of 1976 which also established another instrument, Likoba, to handle banks facing temporary liquidity crises.

Like for the case of French apparatus, the German system is also founded on the correspondence between bank associations and the protection funds. In all of the three cases, albeit, the German funds have financial administrations independent from the respective associations.

As a consequence of their imprinting addressed to avoid uniform and legal regulation, all funds were established on a voluntary basis. The right for members and for their depositors to obtain the funds support does not exist, if a crisis arrives; it means the system does not provide an automatic mechanism of intervention. Furthermore, the kind of intervention is chosen without any defined rule, that is each fund decides how and how extensively to act towards a problem member bank.

Two of the three funds, co-operative banks' and savings banks', are not explicitly aimed at protecting depositors; rather they pursue the protection of their members through preventive actions, loans, subsidies and guarantees. While both of them are organized at regional level – many regional funds exists which support regional banks branches – their mechanism widely differ.

The co-operative banks' fund is a guarantee fund which support banks during liquidity crisis. The members' contributions are annual premiums equal to 0.5 per mill of the granted credits. If necessary the premiums may be increased up to three times their value. The competent regional fund may support members' banks up to 1 million marks. Finally, the support to members may be refused. However, since regional associations are responsible for yearly auditing of member accounts, they have to intervene in order to balance eventual irregularities.

Savings banks are organized as an independent system; they have a central bank and they are mostly owned by local authorities. So that this category of banks has a final guarantor which is credible for all depositors. However, they have established 12 regional protection funds which intervene independently in member banks up to 15 per cent of their total amount when the problem banks are not able to honour their debts or when they are losing their capital. The value of each fund may arrive up to 3 per mill of the member bank assets and single contributions are equal to 0.3 per mill of annual member bank assets.

The commercial banks' fund differs from the others in that it is more explicitly aimed to protect depositors. Although commercial banks' protection programme considers also supporting interventions, it is principally established to intervene in banking failures through pay off procedures up to 30 per cent of banks' liable capital per depositor. The protection is not extensive, interbank deposits, deposits of "involved" persons are excluded. Nevertheless foreign currency deposits and deposits of foreign branches of German banks are covered. Annual single bank contribution which is equal to 0.3 per mill of its deposits may be increased up to 0.6 per mill if it is needed. In this case contributions are related to depositors according to its aim whereas the other funds consider as basis for contribution the granted credits volume. In fact they are just intended to compensate eventual losses on bank credits, rather than to safeguard depositors from losses.

5.2.5 Other EEC Countries: Holland, Belgium, Spain

Holland established a compulsory scheme in 1979 which applies to all banks and credit institutions including branches of foreign banks, while depositors at foreign branches of Dutch banks are not covered.

The system is aimed at protecting small savers and ensuring financial stability. In fact the fund intervenes only to pay off depositors after a failure or a measure of payment suspension.

A co-insurance device is considered, so that deposits are covered up to 35,000 guilders, a limit which is index-linked.

The scheme is not funded, it is virtual. When payments have to be made, the central bank advances payments and apportions them among participating institutions, subject to a maximum annual contribution measured as a ratio of member bank deposits to the whole deposits in the protected banks, the central bank meeting any payment above this level.

Two different voluntary funds were established in Belgium since 1985 to protect commercial banks and savings institutions according to an agreement between the two banking groups and the Institut de Rescompte et de Garantie. Each participating institution contribute yearly up to 0.2 per cent of its deposits and these quotas are redeemable, capitalized after two years if not utilized.

The fund may intervene through pay off only if preventive measures are more expensive or if pay off is indispensable for the financial system.

Each depositor is reimbursed up to 500,000 Belgian francs if the fund has enough resources to meet this ceiling. The indemnity the fund provides is then related to its available resources.

The central bank of Spain and private banks contribute to managing a voluntary guarantee fund which is engaged in preventing bank crises and in insuring deposits. The first type of intervention includes the surveillance activity on a problem bank from the fund, take over operations and finally the possibility of selling troubled banks. When a pay off procedure is undertaken, depositors of all kinds for any class of deposits are protected up to 1.5 million of pesetas.

Annual contributions to the fund are of 0.12 per cent of total deposits for participating banks. The Bank of Spain makes annual contribution equal to that of member banks in aggregate. During a banking crisis the central bank contribution may increase four times.

Separate funds exist which are administrated on virtually identical lines, protecting savings banks and credit co-operatives.

NOTES

1. Taylor (1986) defines securitization as the process of creating financial instruments which act to increase the efficiency with which the capital market function as a financial intermediary.
2. In 1829 the State of New York introduced a protection scheme. In 1831 was the turn of Vermont, in 1834 of Indiana and in 1836 of Michigan. The crisis which occurred in 1937 was an important testing bench for this system. Many of them were swept by the depression of those years, others survived. However, in 1866 every system had ceased to exist because of the concurrence of the so-called "free banks" and because of the settlement of the national banking system which limited the circulation of bank-notes to those of the national banks. In 1866, furthermore, the national system became guarantor of circulating bank-notes protecting them with federal bonds. After the Civil War, deposits became the crucial variable, and the protection systems of that period were intended to safeguard them. So that in 1907 Oklahoma introduced its deposit insurance system, followed by other seven states: Kansas, Nebraska, Texas, Mississippi, South Dakota, North Dakota and Washington. They were compulsory for state banks and provided for a fund which had no limits in protecting depositors. The great depression of 1929, anyway, was so sweeping and wide-spread that no state-basis system was capable of surviving.
3. Elements on present deposit insurance scheme have been gathered by McCarty (1980), proceeding from a conference in Rome (1984), Ocse (1987) and various official sources.
4. The limit was originally set at $2,500. In 1980 it was increased up to $40,000.
5. First adopted in August 1989.

6. Under the Firrea (Financial Institutions Reform, Recovery and Enforcement Act) the assessment rate on Bif-insured and Saif-insured institutions are due to increase respectively to 0.15 per cent and to 0.23 per cent on January 1991. Assimilation of the assessment rates for the two classes of institutions was planned for completion by the end of 1997.
7. If the acquiring bank takes over the "good" assets of the failed institution only, the resolution is termed "clean bank P&A", and if it takes on board all the assets the resolution is termed "whole bank P&A".
8. Examples for direct assistance are the rescue of Continental Illinois in 1984 and of the large Texan holding company M. Corp in 1989.
9. COM(85) 788 final, Official Journal of the European Communities No C346/55.
10. (87/63/EEC), Official Journal of the European Communities No L33/16.
11. Saunders (1983) provides empirical evidence on the effects of public confidence concerning the life-boat experience during the 1973-74 crisis.
12. This ministry decree, dated 27.7.74 was issued when the crisis of the Banca Privata Italiana occurred.

Table 5.1: Synoptic table for deposit insurance schemes

Country	Date	Prevalent Criterion	Condition Membership	Unique Fund	Admin	Financing Scheme	Limits of Coverage	Deposit Covered	Banks' Annual Contribution
USA	1933	insurance	compulsory & voluntary	no	official	contributions from particip. institut.	$100,000	all	0.15% of insured deposits annual premium rateable
Canada	1967	insurance	compulsory	yes	official	contributions from particip. institut.	up to 60,000 can. $ per depositor	all	0.33% of insured deposits annual premium
Japan	1971	insurance	compulsory	yes	semi-official	contrib. part. inst. & Government (1/3)	up to 10m. Yen per depositor	domestic currency	0.012% of insur. deposits annual premium
Britain	1982	insurance	compulsory	no	official	contribuions from particip. institut.	75% of deposits up to £20,000 per ~positor	domestic currency	minimum initial contr. of £10,000, further calls when necessary up to £300,000
Italy	1987	mutualistic & insurance	voluntary	no	private	calls on part. inst in the event of loss Fund ceiling 4 trill	100% on claims to £200m. 75% between 200m. and 800m.	all	variable, tot. amount fund set at 1% of tot. deposits of particip. institutions
France	1980	profession & solidarity	compulsory	yes	private	calls on part. inst. in the event of loss	Ff 0.4m. per depositor	domestic currency	variable, depends on losses annual maximum of Ff10m.
Germany	1966	comm. banks solidarity	voluntary	no	private	contributions from particip. institut.	maximum 30% of bank's liable capital	all	annual premium of 0.03% deposits
Holland		insurance	compulsory	yes	official	calls on part. inst. in the event of loss	per depositor 35,000 guilders per depositor	all	based on % loss to be met sing. cont. 10% own funds

178

Country	Date	Prevalent Criterion	Condition Membership	Unique Fund	Admin	Financing Scheme	Limits of Coverage	Deposit Covered	Banks' Annual Contribution
Belgium	1979	insurance	voluntary	no	official	calls on part. inst. in the event of loss	Bfr 0.5m. per depositor (limited to assets available)	all	0.02% of Bfr liabilities
Spain	1977	insurance	voluntary	yes	official	contrib. part. inst. and Central Bank 1/2	Pta 1,5 m. per depositor	all	0.12% of deposits
Ireland	1989	insurance	compulsory	yes	official	contrib. part inst.	80% of first I£5,000- 70% of next 5,000-50% of next 5,000	domestic currency	0.2% of deposits, min. of I£20,000, no maximum
Switzerland	1984	insurance	voluntary	yes	private	calls on part. inst. in the event of loss	variable, depends on deposit amount	some	variable, depends on banks balances and tot. deposits
Turkey	1983	insurance	compulsory	yes	official	contrib. part. inst.	3m Turkish lire per depositor	sav. dep.	0.5% of deposits
Norway	1961	solidarity	compulsory	yes	official	contrib. part. inst.	variable	all	0.15% of bank's balance
Argentina	1979	insurance	voluntary		official	contrib. part. inst. and Central Bank	100% up 100m arg. dollars 90% above this amount	domestic currency	0.03% of deposits
Chile	1977	guarantee	compulsory		official	financed by Treasury	100 month variable tax units	domestic currency	
India	1978	insurance & guarant.	voluntary		official	contrib. part. inst.	Rs 20,000 for deposits Rs 100,000 for credit guarant.	all	0.04% for deposit insuran. 0.25% of credit guarant.
Lebanon	1967	insurance	compulsory		official	contrib. part inst	Li 30,000	domestic currency	prem. betw. 0.05% – 0.02%
Philippines	1963	insurance	compulsory		official	contrib. part inst	10,000	all	prem. betw 1/18% – 1/12%

Sources: McCarthy (1980); *The Economist* (10th March, 1990); OCSE (1987); Various.

Conclusions

This book has examined the relation existing between banks and deposit insurance schemes. Our focus has been on banks' calling for protection and on deposit insurance effectiveness to achieve this protection notwithstanding the risk taking incentives built in insurance which may serve to exacerbate any tendencies towards banking instability.

Banking is a risky business and the management of risk is the key to success both in operating a bank and supervising a banking system.

In the recent years the likelihood of failure of individual banks has significantly increased because of many factors which modified the risk profile of banking: changes in the financial environment, such as higher and more volatile interest rates and the considerable growth of off-balance-sheet activities of banks; changes in technology, resulting in faster and cheaper transfer of funds among banks and finally increased competition together with a movement towards deregulation.

After a 50 year period of a relatively low rate of failures for banks, during the '80s the number of insolvent banks reached record highs especially in the U.S.A.[1] where the safety net for the financial system is provided with the oldest deposit insurance scheme.

The recrudescence of the banking crises phenomenon as deregulation proceeds and the following implications on the institutional protection apparatus are the setting of the current debate on the effectiveness of deposit insurance.

The United States experience has severely tested the capability of its two federal deposit insurance funds, the Fdic and the Fslic. The Federal Savings and Loan Insurance Corporation has sustained massive losses from the insolvencies of hundred of thrifts and tens of billions of dollars of general Treasury revenues which are necessary to make good the losses in the fund which had previously been financed solely through premiums assessed on thrifts deposits. The Fslic is now abolished with the Federal Deposit Insurance Corporation taking over the Fslic insurance role. The Fdic itself which has sustained much smaller losses is considered to be in poor enough financial condition that its premium assessments are considered to be increased substantially.

The U.S. case is emblematic. It shows the crisis of the pioneering deposit insurance system which has performed as a model for most other schemes introduced in many countries. The present U.S. system crisis might involve other financial systems and then other deposit protection schemes. Furthermore the Fdic's experience focuses on the degeneration the deposit insurance system may be affected by if it departs from its original objectives and if its managing procedures are stressed beyond those convenient for handling a bank failure.

As we have seen, many different deposit insurance schemes operate in a lot of countries. They differ quite considerably from one to another in several aspects and they conformed more or less strictly either to insurance or to mutual assistance criteria, reflecting both local financial environments and historical developments in the countries involved. Whatever the nature of the schemes their objectives are unique: to provide a safe investment vehicle for unsophisticated savers and to stabilize depositories against runs. These micro and macro objectives are a common ground for deposit insurance schemes and one may prevail on the other according to the level of regulation on the banking industry implemented by the authorities and by the different devices which operate in the financial system to preserve its stability.

Deposit insurance is just one of the possible protecting mechanisms which can be introduced in the institutional framework of the financial system. Last resort lending provided by central banks and regulation on banks activities – such as capital ratios, portfolio constraints, reserve requirements and interest ceilings – are the most common devices respectively aimed at providing an extraordinary channel to inject liquidity into a single bank facing temporary difficulties and to control a bank's riskiness.

Every central bank can operate as lender of last resort and the extension and the frequency of this kind of assistance depends on discretionary choices regarding the opportunity to intervene directly into the system involving some cost for the community. On the other hand, regulation owes its fortune as a controlling device to the prevailing trends in the policy either to State intervention or to *laissez-faire*.

If binding regulation is fashionable and many constraints are implemented on banking activities, the introduction of a deposit insurance scheme can be viewed as an attempt to protect depositors from the probable perverse behaviour of banks assuming high risk because of restrictions. Similarly, if central bank Llr function is not well developed, the macro objective of keeping contagious runs from destroying the money supply and the payment system, is the major justification for deposit insurance from the viewpoint of the monetary authorities. So that deposit insurance may be intended to pursue financial stability engendering public confidence in the system.

In our opinion the rationale for deposit insurance has to be founded on the necessity and the opportunity to arrange a mechanism to handle banking failures. Public confidence in the financial system has to be built on the capability of monetary authorities to intervene in time and properly during potential system-wide crises. On the other hand bank behaviour has to be controlled by prudential regulation but in such a way to let banks working like any other competitive firms.

The task is to achieve satisfactory regulation while not cramping the initiative and the adaptation that strengthen the banking industry. This completion is most likely to be achieved if regulatory arrangements evolve in a manner which continue to leave a substantial responsibility with those who are directly involved as market agents, namely the banks and their depositors.

When it is based on a built-in mechanism of coinsurance and on operational procedures aimed at paying-off depositors, deposit insurance is an effecting device in protecting depositors whilst encouraging responsible behaviour.

The provision of a winding-up procedure for insolvent depository institutions, like the deposit insurance, makes failures less likely by making them a real possibility. This means that some institutions may operate in a unsafe manner and regulation and supervision of them are requested. Deposit insurance, from this point of view, does not substitute regulation in controlling banks' behaviour; on the contrary it becomes necessary. However, if depository institutions know they can fail and will be allowed to fail, they may have sufficient incentives to conduct their business in a safe manner.

Furthermore, in the case of a bank insolvency, if the institution is closed and deposit insurance pays off the insured depositors up to a limit, which must be less than the global claims, the crisis is prevented from becoming contagious for other institutions. In this manner the negative effects of a bank failure remain circumscribed and a system-wide runs is averted. To achieve this outcome it is necessary that the coverage extension and the rules for determining closure do not result in de facto protection for equity owners or for the bank management.

The main problem associated with the failure of a bank is represented by the costs involved in it. In the case of a single bank failure the losses suffered by bank's depositors and shareholders are the costs of the probability that the risky business of banking may be unsuccessful. Therefore these costs are to be born by the economic agents involved in the business. On the contrary, if a system-wide crisis causes many banks to fail some social costs are associated with this event. The riskiness of banking is unsettled and the value of the default probability is not more consistent with the risk assumed by depositors and shareholders. In this case, the community which bears the costs and deposit insurance is no more the most convenient instrument to share these costs.

As we have seen it is extraordinarily difficult to determine whether social costs should be included in the premiums for the insurance which are assessed on participating institutions and, how to do that without the knowledge of a well-defined social welfare function.

This reasoning allows us to conclude that deposit insurance must serve as a device limited to end a single bank facing the insolvency problem, whereas monetary authorities have to intervene in the financial system when a potentially wide crisis occurs. Central authorities have the necessary discretionary power to operate in emergency and without any limits. On the contrary, deposit insurance must be explicitly settled ex-ante and must conform its interventions to its scheme in order to be effcctive in protecting unsophisticated savers and in minimising its built-in perverse effects on bank behaviour.

NOTE

1. See for example Jaffee (1989) and Keeley (1990 for US commercial banks increased failures during the '80s.

Bibliography

Akerlof, G.A., (1970), "The Market for Lemons: Quality Uncertainty and the Market Mechanism", *Quarterly Journal of Economics*, 84, 488-500.

Allen, P.R. and Wilhelm, W.J., (1988), "The Impact of the 1980 Depository Institutions, Deregulation and Monetary Control Act on Market Value and Risk: Evidence for Capital Markets", *Journal of Money, Credit and Banking*, August.

Alton G.P., (1985), "Recent Changes in Handling Bank Failure and Their Effects on the Banking Industry", *Federal Reserve Bank of St. Luis, Bulletin*, June, 3-17.

Alton G.P., (1986), "Coping with Bank Failures: Some Lessons from U.S. and U.K.", *Federal Reserve Bank of St. Louis, Economic Review*, 10, December.

Arrow, K.L., (1968), "The Economics of Moral Hazard: Further Comment", *American Economic Review*.

Avery, R.B. and Belton, T.M., (1987) "A Comparison of Risk-Based Capital and Risk-Based Deposit Insurance", *Federal Reserve Bank of Cleveland, Economic Review*, 4, 20-30.

Azaridis C. (1980), "Self-fulfilling Prophecies", *Journal of Economic Theory*, 225 December, 380-396.

Baer, H., (1985), "Private Prices , Public Insurance: the Pricing of Federal Deposit Insurance", *Federal Reserve Bank of Chicago, Economic Perspectives*, September/October, 45-57.

Baer, H. and Brewer E., (1986), "Uninsured Deposit as a Source of Market Discipline: Some New Evidence." *Federal Reserve Bank of Chicago, Economic Perspectives*, September/October, 23-28.

Barnett, R.E., Horvitz P.M. and Silverberg S.C., (1977), "Deposit Insurance. The Present System and Some Alternatives", *The Banking Law Journal*.

Belton, T.M., Gelfand, M.D., Humphrey, D.D., (1987), "Daylight Overdraft and Payment System Risk", *Federal Reserve Bulletin*, November, 839-852.

Bennet, B., (1984), "Bank Regulation and Deposit Insurance: Controlling the Fdic's Losses", *Federal Reserve Bank of San Francisco, Economic Review*, 2, Spring, 16-30.

Benston, G.J., (1983), "Deposit Insurance and Bank Failures", *Federal Reserve Bank of Atlanta, Economic Review*, March, 4-17.

Benston, J., Eisenbeis, R.A., Horvitz, P.M., Kane, E. and Kaufman, G.G., (1986), *Perspectives on Safe and Sound Banking: Past, Present and Future*, the MIT Press, Cambridge.

Benston, G.J. and Kaufman G.G., (1988),"Regulating Bank Safety and Performance", in Haralf, W.S. and Kushmeider, R.M.,(eds).

Bernanke, B.S., (1983) "Non Monetary Effects of the Financial Crisis on the Propagation of the Great Depression", *American Economic Review*, June, 257-76.

Bernheim, D.B., (1988), "The Crisis in Deposit Insurance Issues and Options", *Banking Research Center Working Paper*, n.163, J.L. Kellog Graduate School of Management, Northwestern University, October.

Bianchi, T., (1986), "Brevi considerazioni sul Fondo Interbancario di tutela dei depositi", Banca Notizie.

Bierwag, G.O. and Kaufman G.G., (1983), "A Proposal for Federal Deposit Insurance with Risk Sensitive Premiums", *Federal Reserve Bank of Chicago, Economic Review*, March, 223-242.

Biffis, P., (1986), "La tutela dei depositi bancari", *Note Economiche*.

Bignardi, F., (1987), "Il Fondo Interbancario serve a consolidare la fiducia della clientela", *Parabancaria*, Dicembre.

Bingham, T.R.G., (1984),"Banking and Monetary Policy", OECD.

Black, F. and Scholes, M., (1973), "The Pricing Options and Corporate Liabilities", *Journal of Political Economy*, May/June, 637-654.

Blair, R.D. and Heggestad, A.A., (1978), "Bank Portfolio Regulation and the Probability of Bank Failure", Journal *of Money, Credit and Banking*, February, 88-93.

Boyd, J.H. and Prescott, E.C., (1986), "Financial Intermediary Coalitions", *Journal of Political Economy*, 88, 146-173.

Brumbaugh, R.D. and Hemel, E.I., (1984), "Federal Deposit Insurance as a Call Option: Implication for Depository Institutions", *Research Working Paper*, n.116, Washington D.C.: Federal Home Loan Bank Board, Office of Policy and Economic Research, October.

Bryant, J., (1980), "A Model of Bank Reserves, Bank Runs and Deposit Insurance", *Journal of Banking and Finance*, n.4, 335-344.

Bryant, J. and Wallace, N., (1980), "Open Market Operations in a Model of Regulated, Insured Intermediaries, *Journal of Political Economy*, 88, 146-173.

Burket, P., (1990), " The Competitive Payments System: Some Stability Problems", *Journal of Post Keynesian Economics*, Summer, 572-590.

Buser, S.A., Chen, A.H. and Kane, E.J., (1981), "Federal Deposit Insurance, Regulatory Policy and Optimal Bank Capital", *Journal of Finance*, March, 51-60.

Calomiris, C.W., (1989), "Deposit Insurance: Lessons from the Record", *Federal Reserve Bank of Chicago, Economic Perspectives*, May/June, 10-30.

Calomiris C.W., (1990), "Is Deposit Insurance Necessary? : A Historical Perspective", *Journal of Economic History*, June.

Calomiris, C.W. and Gorton, G.G., (1990), " The Origins of Banking Panics Models, Facts, and Banking Regulation", Wharton School, University of Pennsylvanya, n. 11.

Cammarano, G., (1979), In La Tutela del risparmio Bancario, AA.VV.

Campbell, T.S. and Glenn, D., (1984), "Deposit Insurance in a Deregulated Environment", *Journal of Finance*, 39, 775-785.

Cargill, T.E. and Garcia, G.G., (1985), *Financial Reform in the 1980's.*

Carns, F.S., (1989)," Should the $100,000 Deposit Insurance Limit Be Changed?", *Fdic Banking Review*, Spring/Summer, 11-19.

Carroll, E. and Rolnick, A., (1985), "After Penn Square: The Insurance Dilemma", in Proceeding of a Conference on Bank Structure and Competition, Federal Reserve Bank of Chicago.

Chan, Y.S. and Mak, K.T., (1985), "Depositors' Welfare, Deposit Insurance and Deregulation", *Journal of Finance*, July, 959-974.

Chan, Y.S., Stuart, I.G. and Anjan V.T., (1988)," Is Fairly Priced Deposit Insurance Possible?", *Banking Research Centre Working Paper*, n.152, J.L. Kellog Graduate School of Management, Northwestern University, October.

Chari, V.V., (1989) "Banking Without Deposit Insurance or Bank Panics: Lessons From a Model of the U.S. National Banking System", *Federal Reserve Bank of Minneapolis, Quarterly Review*, 3-19.

Chari, V.V and Jagannathan, R., (1988),"Banking Panics, Information and Rational Expectations Equilibrium", *Journal of Finance*, 43, July, 749-761.

Ciocca, P., (1981), *Interesse e profitto, Saggi sul sistema creditizio*, Bologna.

Claassen, E.M., (1985), "The Lender of Last Resort Function in the Context of National and International Crisis", *Weltwirtschaftliches* Archiv, 217-237.

Class D. and Shell K., (1983)," Do Sunspots Matters?" *Journal of Political Economy*, 91, April, 193-227.

Cumming, C.M., (1985), "Federal Deposit Insurance and Deposit of Foreign Branches of U.S. Banks", *Federal Reserve Bank of New York, Quarterly Review*, 10, 30-38.

Cummins, J.D., (1988), "Risk-Based Premius for Insurance Guaranty Founds", *Journal of Finance*, September, 823-839.

Darrough, M.N. and Stoughton, N.M., (1986), "Moral Hazard and Adverse Selection: The Question of Financial Structure", *Journal of Finance*, June.

De Cecco, M. and Giovannini, A., (1989), *A European Central Bank? Perspectives on Monetary Unification after ten Years of Ems*, Cambridge, Cambridge University Press.

De Felice, G., Masciandaro, D. and Porta, A., (1988), "Evoluzione del sistema bancario nella struttura finanziaria e problemi di regolamentazione", in Cesarini, F., Monti, M. and Onado, M., (eds), Banca e Mercato, Il Mulino, Bologna.

Diamond, D.W., (1984), "Financial Intermediation and Delegated Monitoring", *Review of Economic Studies*, July, 393-414.

Diamond, D.W. and Dybvig, P.H., (1983), "Bank Runs, Deposit Insurance and Liquidity", *Journal of Political Economy*, 91, n.3, 401-419.

Diamond, D.W. and Dybvig, P.H. (1986), "Banking Theory, Deposit Insurance and Bank Regulation", *Journal of Finance*, July, 55-68.

Dince, R.R., (1986), "Ispezioni bancarie negli Stati Uniti. Nuove tecniche per un mondo che cambia", Banca, Impresa e Societé, 2.

Dietrich, J.K. and James, C., (1983), "Regulation and the Determination of Bank Capital Changes: A Note", *Journal of Finance*, December, 1651-1658

Dini, L., (1983)," Handling of Bank Crises in Italy", in Banca d'Italia, *Documenti* n.107.

Dudley, W.C., (1986), *Controlling Risk on Large-Dollar Wire Transfer System, in Technology and Regulation of Financial Markets*, Saunders A. and White L.J. (eds), Lexington Book.

Dufey, G. and Giddy, I.H., (1984), "Eurocurrency Deposit Risk", *Journal of Banking and Finance*, June.

Eisenbeis, R.A., (1985), "Market Discipline and the Prevention of Bank Problems and Failure", *Issues in Bank Regulation*, Winter.

Ely, B., (1985), "Yes, Private Sector Depositor Protection is Viable Alternative to Federal deposit Insurance", *Proceedings of a Conference on Bank Structure and Competition, Federal Reserve Bank of Chicago*.

England, C., (1985), "A Proposal for Introducing Private Deposit Insurance", *in Proceedings of a Conference on Bank Structure and Competition, Federal Reserve Bank of Chicago*.

Fama, E.F., (1980), "Banking in the Theory of Finance", *Journal of Monetary Economics*, January, 39-57.

Fazio, A., (1985), "La tutela dei depositi bancari", in Banca d'Italia, *Bollettino Economico*, n. 4.

Fdic, (1983), *Agenda for Reform, A report on Deposit Insurance to the Congress from the Federal Home Loan Bank Board*, Washington D.C.

Fdic, (1983), *Deposit Insurance in a Changing Environment. A study submitted to Congress by Federal Deposit Insurance Corporation*, Washington D.C.

Fdic, (1984), *The first Fifty Years*, Washington D.C.

Fdic, (1985), *Discussion Paper on Risk-related Deposit Insurance, American Banker*, 23/9.

FdicC, (1989), *Deposit Insurance for the Nineties: Meeting the Challenge, A stuff Study*, Washington, January.

Field,W., (1985), "The Case for 100 per cent Deposit Insurance", *Bankers Magazine*, U.S., November.

Flannery, M.J., (1982), "Deposit Insurance Creates Need for Bank Regulation", *Federal Reserve Bank of Philadelphia, Business Review*, January/February, 17-27.

Friedman, B. and Formuzis, P., (1985), "Bank Capital: the Deposit Protection Incentive", *Journal of Bank Research*, Autumn.

Friedman, M. and Schwartz, A.J., (1963), *A Monetary History of United States, 1867-1960*.

Furlong, F., (1984) "A View on Deposit Insurance Coverage", *Federal Reserve Bank of San Francisco, Economic Review,* Spring, 31-37.

Gibson, W., (1972), "Deposit Insurance in the United States: Evaluation and Reform", *Journal of Financial and Quantitative Analysis,* March, 1575-1595.

Garber, P.M. and Grilli, V.U. (1989), " Banks Runs in Open Economies and the International Transmission of Panics", *Journal of International Economics,* 27, 165-175.

Gilbert, R.A., (1985), "Recent Changes in Handling Bank Failures and Their Effects on the Banking Industries", *Federal Reserve Bank of St. Louis, Economic Review,* June/July, 21-28.

Gilbert, R.A., (1989), "Payment System Risk: What Is It and What Will Happen if We Tray to Reduce It?", *Federal Reserve Bank of St. Louis, Economic Review,* January/February, 3-17.

Golembe, C.H., (1960), "The Deposit Insurance Legislation of 1933", *Political Science Quarterly.*

Goodhart, C., (1975), *Money, Information and Uncertainty,* McMillan Press ltd, Hong Kong.

Goodhart, C., (1985), The Evolution of Central Bank.

Goodhart, C., (1986), Why Do We Need a Central Bank?, Banca d'Italia, *Temi di discussione,* n.57, January.

Goodhart, C., (1987), *Bank Insolvency and Deposit Insurance: a Proposal,* Offprint.

Goodhart, C., (1987), "Financial Regulation and Supervision: a Review of Three Books", *National Westminster, Bank Quarterly Review,* August.

Goodhart, C., (1988), "The Regulatory Debate in London", *LSE Financial Markets Group, Special Paper Series,* n.7.

Goodman, L.S., (1983), "Fixed Rate Deposit Insurance: A Reexamination", *Federal Reserve Bank of New York, Working Paper.*

Goodman, L.S. (1984), "The Economics of Deposit Insurance", Offprint.

Goodman, L.S. and Santomero, A.M., (1986), "A Variable-Rate Deposit Insurance: a Reexamination", *Journal of Banking and Finance,* 203-218.

Goodman, L.S. and Shaffer, S., (1984) "The Economics of Deposit Insurance: A Critical Evaluation of Proposed Reforms", *Federal Reserve Bank of New York, Quarterly Review, Research Paper,* August, 145-162.

Gorton, B.G., (1985), "Clearinghouses and the Origin of Central Banking in the United States", *The Journal of Economic History,* 45, June, 277-283.

Gorton, B.G., (1987), "Bank Suspension of Convertibilities", *Journal of Monetary Economics,* March, 15, 177-193.

Gorton, B.G., (1988), "Banking Panics and Business Cycles", *Oxford Economic Papers,* 40, December, 751-781.

Gorton, B.G., (1989), "Self-Regulating Bank Coalitions", *The Warton School, University of Pennsylvanya, unpublished working paper.*

Gorton, B.G. and Haubrich J.G., (1987), "Bank Deregulation, Credit, Markets, and the Control of Capital", Canergie, *Rochester Conference Series on Public Policy,* 26, 289-334.

Gorton, B.G. and Mullineaux, D.J., (1987), "The Joint Production of Confidence: Endogenous Regulation and Nineteenth Century Commercial-Bank

Clearinghouses", *Journal of Money, Credit and Banking*, 19, November, 457-468.

Gorton, B.G. and Pennacchi G. (1990), "Financial Intermediation and Liquidity Creation", *Journal of Finance*, n.45, 49-72.

Greenbaum, S.I. and Thakor, A.V., (1987), "Bank Funding Modes: Securitization Versus Deposits", *Journal of Banking and Finance*, September.

Greenspan, A., (1988), "Innovation and Regulation of Banks in 1990s", *Federal Reserve Bulletin*, 784-787.

Griffith-Jones, S. and Lipton, M., (1984)," International Lenders of Last Resort: Are Changes Required?", Institute of Development Studies, Sussex, March.

Grubel, H.G., (1979), "A Proposal for the Establishment of an International Deposit Insurance Corporation", *Essays in International Finance*, n.133, Princeton, N.J, July.

Guttentag, J.M. and Herring, R.J., (1988), "Restructuring Depository Institutions", *Wharton Program in International Banking and Finance, University of Pennsylvania*, January.

Hall, M.J.B., (1987), "The Deposit Protection Scheme: The case for Reform", *National Westminster Bank Quarterly Review*, August, 45-54.

Hall, M.J.B., (1991), "The Reform of Federal Deposit Insurance: The Options", *Banca Nazionale del Lavoro, Economic Review*, 441-458.

Hannan, T.H. and Hnwech, G.A., (1988), "Bank Insolvency Risk and the Market for Large Certificates of Deposit", *Journal of Money, Credit and Banking*, 20, May, 203-212.

Haubrich, J.G. and King, R.G., (1990), "Banking and Insurance", *Journal of Monetary Economics*, 26, December, 361-386.

Heinkel, R., (1985), " Deposit Welfare, Deposit Insurance and Deregulation in Discussion", *Journal of Finance*, July.

Herring, R.J. and Vankudre, P., (1987), "Growth Opportunities and Risk-taking by Financial Intermediaries", *Journal of Finance*, July, 583-599.

Herring, R.J. and Vankudre, P., (1985), "The moral Hazard Constraint on the Pricing of Deposit Insurance", *Brookings Discussion Papers International Economics*, November.

Hicks, J., (1989), *A Market Theory of Money*, Clarendon Press, Oxford.

Horvitz, P.M., (1983), "The Case Against Risk-Adjusted Deposit Insurance Premiums", *Housing Finance Review*, July, 270-281.

Horvitz, P.M., (1986), "The Case Against Risk Related Deposit Insurance Premium", in Gardener, E.P.M., Allen and Unwin, *UK Banking Supervision Evolution, Practice and Issues*, London.

Huertas, P.M. and Stauber, R., (1986) Deposit Insurance: Overhaul or Tune-up ?", *Issues in Bank Regulation*, Winter.

Humphrey, D.B., (1976), "100% Deposit Insurance: What Would it Cost?", *Journal of Bank Research*, Autumn.

Humphrey D.B., (1986), *Payment Finality and Risk of Settlement Failure, in Technology and Regulation of Financial Markets*, Saundres A. and White L.J. (eds), Lexington Book.

Humphrey, D.B., (1989) "Market Responses to Pricing Fedwire Daylight Overdrafts", *Federal Reserve Bank of Richmond, Economic Review*, May/June, 23-34.

Humphrey, D.B. and Marquard, J.C., (1987), "Daylight Overdrafts and Payment System Risk", *Federal Reserve Bullettin*, November.

Isaac, W.M., (1984), "International Deposit Insurance Systems", *Issues in Bank Regulation*, Summer.

Jaffee, D.M., (1989), "Symposium on Federal Deposit Insurance for S&L Institution", *Journal of Economic Perspectives*, Fall.

Jacklin, C.J. (1988), "Banks and Risk Sharing: Instabilities and Coordination", *Working Paper No. 185, Center for Research in Security Prices, Graduate School of Business, The University of Chicago*.

Jacklin, C.J. and Bhattacharya, S., (1988), "Distinguishing Panics and Information Based Bank Runs: Welfare and Policy Implications", *Journal of Political Economy*, n. 96, 568-592.

Kahane, Y., (1987), "Capital Adequacy and the Regulation of Financial Intermediaries", *Journal of Banking and Finance*, 207-218.

Kanatas, G., (1986), "Deposit Insurance and Discount Window: Pricing under Asymetric Information", *Journal of Finance*, July, 437-450.

Kane, E.J., (1983), *A Six Point Programme for Deposit Insurance Reform*, Washington D.C.

Kane, E.J., (1985), *The Gathering Crisis in Federal Deposit Assurance*, The MIT Press, Cambridge.

Kane, E.J., (1986), "Appearance and Reality in Deposit Insurance: The Case for Reform", *Journal of Banking and Finance*, 10, 175-188.

Kane, E.J., (1989), "The High Cost of Incompletely Funding the FSLIC's Shortage of Explicit Capital", *Journal of Economic Perspectives*, Fall.

Kareken, J.H., (1983), " The First Step in Bank Deregulation : What About the Fdic?", *American Economic Review*, May, 198-203.

Kareken, J.H., (1986), "Federal Bank Regulatory Policy: A Description and Some Observation", *Journal of Business*, 59, 3-48.

Kareken, J.H., (1990), "Deposit Insurance Reform; or, Deregulation is the Cart, Not the Horse", *Federal Reserve Bank of Minneapolis, Quarterly Review*, Winter, 3-11, reprint.

Kareken, J.H. and Wallance, N., (1978), "Deposit Insurance and Bank Regulation: a Partial Equilibrium Exposition", *Journal of Business*, July, 413-438.

Kaufman, G.G., (1978), "Federal Bank Regulatory Policy: Comment on Kareken", *Journal of Business*.

Kaufman, G.G., (1988), "Bank Runs: Causes, Benefits, and Costs", *Cato Journal*, vol. 7, n. 3, Winter, 559-587.

Keeley, M.C., (1990), "Deposit Insurance, Risk, and Market Power in Banking", *American Economic Review*, December, 1183-1200.

Keeton, W.R., (1984), "Deposit Insurance and Deregulation of Deposit Rates", *Federal Reserve Bank of Kansas City, Economic Review*, April.

Keeton, W.R., (1986)," Deposit Deregulation, Credit Availability and Monetary Policy", *Federal Reserve of Kansas City, Economic Review*, June, 26-42.

Kim, D. and Santomero, A.M., (1988), "Risk in Banking and Capital Regulation", *Journal of Finance*, 5, 1214-1233.

King, M. and Goodhart,C., (1988), "Financial Stability and the Lender of Last Resort Function: a Note", *LSE Financial Markets Group Special Paper Series*, n.2.

Klein, M.A., (1971), "A Theory of Banking Firm", *Journal of Money, Credit and Banking*, May, 205-218.

Kreps, C.H. and Wacht, R.F., (1971), " A more Constructive Role for Deposit Insurance", *Journal of Finance*, 26, May, 605-614.

Kuprianov, A. and Mengle, D.L., (1989), " The Future of Deposit Insurance: An Analysis of the Alternatives", *Federal Reserve Bank of Richmond, Economic Review*, May/June, 3-15.

Lane, D. and Lawrence, G., (1981),"Some Simulation-Based Estimates of Commercial Bank Deposit Insurance", in Maisel, S.J. (ed.), *Risk and Capital Adequacy in Commercial Banks*, The University of Chicago Press.

Laurent, R.D., (1981), "Reserve Requirements, Deposit Insurance and Monetary Control", *Journal of Money, Credit and Banking*, 13, 314-324.

Litan, R.E., (1987), *What Should Banks Do?*, The Brookings Institute, Washington, D.C.

Macchiati, A., (1990), "Assicurazione dei Depositi e Crisi Bancarie in Italia", Banche e Banchieri, Gennaio, 29-45.

Marcus, A.J., (1984), "Deregulation and Bank Financial Policy", *Journal of Banking and Finance*, 81, 557-564.

Marcus, A.J. and Shaked, I., (1984), "The Valuation of FDIC Deposit Insurance Using Option Pricing Estimates", *Journal of Money, Credit and Banking*, November, 446-460.

Marlin, J.A., (1969), "Bank Deposit Insurance", *Banker Magazine*, September.

Mayer, T., (1962), "Is the Portfolio Control of Financial Institutions Justified?", *Journal of Finance*, May, 311-317.

Mayer, T., (1965), "A Graduated Deposit Insurance Plan", *Review of Economics and Statistics*, February, 114-116.

McCarthy, I.S., (1980), " Deposit Insurance: Theory and Practice", *IMF Stuff paper.*

McCormick, J.M. and Moynihan, J.P., (1985), "The Developing Spiral of Risk Created by Bank Capital Regulation", *American Banker*, 26th November.

McCulloch, J.H., (1985), "Interest-Risk Sensitive Deposit Insurance Premia: Stable ACH Estimates", *Journal of Banking and Finance*, March, 137-156.

McCulloch, J.H., (1986), "Bank Regulation and Deposit Insurance", *Journal of Business*, vol. 59, 79-85.

McKenzie G.W., (1989), "The Theory of Financial Market Regulation", Oxford MSG Conference, September, 19-21.

McMahon, C.W., (1977), "Central Banks on Regulations and Lenders of Last Resort: A View from the United Kingdom", *Federal Reserve Bank of Boston, Key Issues in International Banking*, October.

Merton, R.C., (1977), "An Analytic Derivation of the Cost of Deposit Insurance and Loan Guarantees", *Journal of Banking and Finance*, June, 3-11.

Merton, R.C., (1978), "On the Cost of Deposit Insurance When There Are Surveillance Costs", *Journal of Business*, 51, July, 439-452.

Merrick, J.J. and Saunders, A., (1985), "Bank Regulation and Monetary Policy", *Journal of Money, Credit and Banking*, November, 691-717.

Miles, J.A. and Kim. T., (1988), "On the Valuation of Fdic Deposit Insurance: An Empirical Study of the Banking System", *Quarterly Journal of Business and Economy*, Autumn.

Minervini, G., (1987), "Note sull'assicurazione dei depositi bancari", in *Banche in crisi 1960-1985*, Laterza.

Mingo, J.J., (1975), "Regulatory Influence on Bank Capital Investiment", *Journal of Finance*, September, 1111-1122.

Mingo, J.J. and Wolkowitz, B., (1977),"The Effects of Regulation on Bank Balance Sheet Decision", *Journal of Finance*, 5, 1605-1616.

Miron J.A., (1986), "Financial Panics, the Seasonality of the Nominal Interests Rate and the Founding of the Fed", *American Economic Review*, 76(1), March, 125-140.

Morelli, G., (1986) "Payment System in Eleven Developed Countries", *Journal of Bank Review*.

Muller, B., (1981), "Deposit Insurance", ICBS.

Murton, A.J., (1989),"Bank Intermediation, Bank Runs and Deposit Insurance", *Fdic Banking Review*, Spring/Summer, 1-10.

Nastasi, V., (1988), *Crisi Bancarie e tutela dei depositanti*, Il Mulino.

Nelson, R.W., (1989), "Management Versus Economic Condition as Contributors to the Recent Increase in Bank Failures", in Stone, C.C. (ed), *Financial Risk : Theory, Evidence and Implications,* Kluwer Academic Publishers.

Nicosia, B., (1987), "Il Fondo Interbancario di tutela dei Depositi", Bancaria, n.12.

Onado, M., (1984), "Concorrenza e Stabilité nelle aziende di Credito", Banca, *Impresa e Societé*, n.3.

Parravicini,G., (1985), "La Garanzia dei Depositi", *Associazione per lo Sviluppo degli Studi di Banca e Borsa*, quaderno n.66.

Parrillo, F., (1986), Assicurazione e garanzia dei Depositi Bancari nella Comunité Europea, Université di Roma La Sapienza, Facolté di Economia e Commercio e Commercio, Corso di perfezionamento in discipline bancarie, April.

Padoa-Schioppa, T., (1988), *La Moneta, La Politica Economica e L'Europa,* Bruxelles.

Pauly, G. (1968), "The Economics of Moral Hazard: Comment", *American Economic Review*, June.

Pecchioli, R.M., (1987), *Le Controle Prudential des Banques*, OECD.

Peltzman, S., (1970), "Capital Investiment in Commercial Banking and its Relationship to Portfolio Regulation", *Journal of Political Economy*, January/ February, 1-26.

Penati, A. and Protopapadakis, A., (1986), " The Effect of Implicit Deposit Insurance on Bank Portfolios Choices with an Application to International Overexposure", *Federal Reserve Bank of Philadelphia, Department of research, Working Paper* n. 86-16.

Pennacchi, G.G., (1983), "Valuing Variable and Fixed Rate Deposit Insurance for Intermediaries Subject to Interest Rate Risk", *Massachusetts Institute of Technology, Department of Economics, Working Paper*, December.

Pennacchi, G.G, (1987), "Alternative Forms of Deposit Insurance: Pricing and Bank Incentive Issues", *Journal of Banking and Finance*, June, II, 291-309.

Pyle, D.H., (1983), "Pricing Deposit Insurance: The Effects of Mismeasurement", *Federal Reserve Bank of San Francisco, Working Paper*, October.

Pyle, D.H., (1984), "Deregulation and Deposit Insurance Reform", *Federal Reserve of San Francisco, Economic Review*, Spring, 5-15.

Pyle, D.H., (1986) "Capital Regulation and Deposit Insurance, *Journal of Banking and Finance*, 10, 189-201.

Poslewaite, A. and Vives, X., (1987), "Bank Runs as an Equilibrium Phenomenon", *Journal of Political Economy*, 95, 485-491.

Ramakrishnan, R.T. and Thakor, A.V., (1984), "Information Reliability and Theory of Financial Intermediation", *Review of Economic Studies*, July, 415-432.

Redburn, F.S., (1988), "Never Lost a Penny: An Assessment of Federal Deposit Insurance", *Journal of Policy*, Annal Manage, Fall.

Revell, S.R.S., (1980), "The Complementary Nature of Competition and Regulation in the Financial Sector", *Revue de la Banque*.

Revell, S.R.S., (1981), "The Regulation of Banks and the New English Banking Law", *Revue de la Banque*.

Revell, S.R.S., (1985), "Rischio Bancario e Assicurazione dei Depositi", *Banca Impresa e Societé*, n.3.

Ronn, E.I. and Verma, A.K., (1986), "Pricing Risk-Adjusted Deposit Insurance: an Option-Based Model", *Journal of Finance*, September, 871-895.

Russo, D, (1990), "Il Controllo dei Rischi nei Sistemi di Pagamento", in *Banca d'Italia*, Atti del Convegno "Il Sistema dei Pagamenti Italiano: Pogetti in Corso e Prospettive di Sviluppo", Marzo.

Ruta, G., (1970), *Rilievi critici sull'opportunuté di introdurre in Italia un sistema di assicurazione dei depositi bancari, in Studi in onore di A. Donati*.

Samuelson, P., (1985), "An Exact Consumption-Loans Model of Interest with or without the Social Contrivance of Money", *Journal of Political Economy*, 66, 467-482.

Santomero, A.M. and Vinso, J.D., (1977), "Estimating the Probability of Failure for Commercial Banks and the Banking System", *Journal of Banking and Finance*, October, 185-205.

Santomero, A.M. and Watson, R.D., (1977), "Determining an Optimal Capital Standard for the Banking Industry", Journal of Finance, 4, 1267-1281.

Schwartz, A.J.,(1987), "The Lender of Last Resort and Federal Safety", *Journal of Financial Services Research*, September, 1-18.

Schwartz, A.J., (1988), "Bank Runs and Deposit Insurance Reform", *Cato Journal*, Winter, 589-594.

Scott, (1987), "The Defective Design of Federal Deposit Insurance", *Contemporary Policy Issue*, January.

Scott, K.J., (1989)," Deposit Insurance and Bank Regulation: The Policy Choices", *Business Lawyer*, May.

Sharpe, W.F., (1978), "Bank Capital Adequancy, Deposit Insurance and Security Values", *Journal of Financial and Quantitative Analysis*, 13, November, 701-718.

Short, E.D. and O'Driscoll, G.P., (1983), "Deregulation and Deposit Insurance", *Federal Reserve Bank of Dallas, Economic Review*, 11-22.

Silveberger, S.C., (1985),"Resolving Large Bank Problems and Failures", *Issues in Bank Regulation*, Winter.

Skiller, F.L., (1982), "Federal Deposit Insurance Corporation and the Failed Bank : the Past Decade", *The Banking Law Journal*.

Solow, R.M., (1982), "On the Lender of Last Resort", in *Financial Crises-Theory, History and Policy*, Kindleberger C.P., Laffaurge J.P., Maison des Sciences de l'Homme and Cambridge University Press.

Tallman, E., (1988), "Some Unanswered Questions About Bank Panics", *Federal Reserve Bank of Atlanta, Economic Review*, 73, November/December, 2-21.

Tarantola Ronchi, A.M., (1986), "L'Assicurazione dei Depositi in USA", Banca, *Impresa e Societé*, V.

Timberlake, R.H., (1984), "The Central Banking Role of Clearing House Associations", *Journal of Money, Credit and Banking*, February, 1-15.

Tobin, J., (1987), "A Case for Preserving Regulatory Distinctions", *Challenge*.

Tobin, J., (1956), "The Interest-Elasticity of Transaction Demand for Cash", *Review of Economics and Statistics*, 38, August, 241-247.

Tussing, A.D., (1967), "The Case for Bank Failure", *Journal of Law and Economics*, October, 129-147.

Vaubel, R., (1983), "The Moral Hazard of IMF Lending", *The World Economy*, vol.6.

Vella, F., (1985), L'assicurazione ai depositi e l'azione di vigilanza : il caso della Federal Deposit Insurance Corporation, in Profili di Concorrenza e di Integrazione fra Attivité Bancaria e Attivit´ Assicurativa, Milano, Giuffré.

Waldo, D.G., (1985), "Bank Runs, the Deposit-Currency Ratio and the Interest Rate", *Journal of Monetary Economics*, 15, 269-278.

Walker, D.A., (1983), "Regulation in Financial Markets", *Bank of England Quarterly Bulletin*, December, 499-501.

Wallace, N., (1988), "Another Attempt to Explain an illiquid Banking System: The Diamond and Dybving Model with Sequential Services Taken Seriously", *Federal Reserve Bank of Minneapolis, Quarterly Review*, Fall, 3-16.

Walsh, C.E., (1984), "Liquidity Constraints", *Department of Economics, Princeton University, Working Paper*.

White, L.J., (1989), "The Reform of Federal Deposit Insurance", *Journal of Economic Perspectives*, Fall, 11-19.

Williamson, S.D., (1987), "Recent Developments in Modeling Financial Intermediation", *Federal Reserve Bank of Minneapolis, Quarterly Review*, Summer, 19-29.

Woodward, S., (1988), "A Transaction Cost Analysis of Banking Activity and Deposit Insurance", *Cato Journal*, Winter, 683-799.

Index

203